The
TEACHER'S WAY

The Teacher's Way

Teaching and the Contemplative Life

Maria Lichtmann

PAULIST PRESS
New York/Mahwah, N.J.

Cover design by Sharyn Banks

Library of Congress Cataloging-in-Publication Data

Lichtmann, Maria R., 1945-
   The teacher's way : teaching and the contemplative life / Maria Lichtmann.
     p. cm.
   Includes bibliographical references.
   ISBN 0-8091-4303-8 (alk. paper)
   1. Contemplation. 2. Teaching. I. Title.

BV5091.C7L53 2005
248.3—dc22

                                    2004022084

Published by Paulist Press
997 Macarthur Boulevard
Mahwah, New Jersey 07430

www.paulistpress.com

Printed and bound in the
United States of America

CONTENTS

CONTENTS

Preface

Our professional lives these days are lived on the brink of despair. If we are drawn to a book that promises to assuage the damage of our life at work, too often that resource is merely a kidnapped artifact of some ravaged foreign culture, a quick fix of spa spirituality (not that I would pass up a hot tub!). Rarely is a book a true companion on the way, extending the friendship of a fellow-seeker who has lived the life and chooses to walk with us in hospitality. Maria Lichtmann's roots are deep in the genetics of the Judaeo-Christian contemplative life. She has pondered the treasures of these traditions and brings to them a lifetime of practice to her attentive teaching and writing. She leads us here to springs that will not fail.

If introducing a book is rather like writing an invitation to gather like-minded people together, then it is a pleasure to bring readers to this delicate and dangerous book. Maria Lichtmann's transformative vision subverts the status quo and puts every educational theory up for grabs. I love this about it. Has the radical and oppositional quality of contemplative practice ever been so clearly explained? "Paradoxically," Lichtmann writes, "transformation happens only when formation breaks down." This sentence tersely challenges me to understand why the work of contemplative teachers puts us so painfully at odds with the educational culture of expediency, mastery, control, and power.

One cannot come away from this book without a deeper comprehension of why contemplation has been marginalized by most educational establishments. (For my part, I have lived a teaching life too naïve or too busy to figure this out.) Lichtmann repeatedly quotes one of my favorite contemplative apologists, Constance Fitzgerald, OCD, who warns that spiritual progress comes at the price of doubt and breakdown. Not to know that fact is productive of bitterness. To surrender intelligently to the process lets one wear, instead, a little secret smile on the face of the soul.

—*Mary Rose O'Reilley*

Acknowledgments

For the many people who have encouraged and nurtured this project along the way, I give thanks. For conversations about teaching that took place in very different venues: with the Fellows of the Lilly Fellows Program at Valparaiso University, with faculty at the President's Faculty Institute at Loyola Marymount University who first responded to the ideas that form the basis of this book, with Parker and Sharon Palmer over tea and scones in my living room, and with faculty in the Inner Landscape of Teaching groups at Berea College. For a Faculty-Student Research Grant from Berea College, which enabled me to have the research support of an exceptional student, Linda Proeschel, not the least of whose talents was her ready laughter and enjoyment of the work. For those who read early drafts while the manuscript grew from an article to a book, among them Kate Brinko, Chuck Claxton, Connie Green, Libby Jones, Charlene Lichtmann, Mary Rose O'Reilley, Parker Palmer, Peggy Rivage-Seul, Jan Schmidt, and Robert Schneider. For the incalculable assistance of my two editors at Paulist Press, Kathleen Walsh, who read several drafts, bringing it out of its most amorphous state into some semblance of structure, and Christopher Bellitto, who carried it through to completion with gentle and timely prodding. For those who gave me technical aid in overcoming my near panic at the task of converting the manuscript from one word-processing program to another, my nephew, Daniel Hertrich, and Mary Beth McKee. Most of all, I thank my students over the nearly thirty years of my teaching. Each and all have been my teacher far more than they know. Finally, I dedicate this book to my mother, Louceil Lichtmann, who first as a Benedictine nun and college professor (in two departments, music and classics) and then as a married woman and teacher of fourth-graders, modeled the exemplary teacher. Her lively faith in God and love for each of her students continue to inspire me today.

Introduction

A movement that connects spirituality and education is growing today, judging from the appearance of a number of books and discussions concerned with a more contemplative approach to teaching and learning.[1] In conferences with titles such as "Teaching from Within: Vocation, Practice, and Transformation" and "Education as Transformation: Religious Pluralism, Spirituality, and Higher Education," the 1998 conference at Wellesley College, we hear voices calling for reintegration of these once-severed realms. More educators are noticing the neglect of students' "inner" development. This is especially true in public education, where religion as a subject has been all but outlawed.

Teachers' own spiritual yearnings also cry out for realization. Speaking to this hunger for the spiritual dimension of teaching, Parker Palmer's *To Know As We Are Known,* as well as his more recent *The Courage to Teach,*[2] have energized teachers all over the country. In response to feelings of spiritual depletion felt by many teachers today, other writers on the art of teaching such as Maria Harris, bell hooks, and Mary Rose O'Reilley have made strong connections between teaching and the life of the spirit.

This book continues the larger conversation going on in educational circles reconnecting education with the life of the spirit. It aims to uncover a sense of teaching as a *spiritual* practice. The word *spiritual* as applied to anything is simply that element brought into unity with the whole. The spiritual life is human life enlivened, lived to the *nth* power, so that a spirituality of teaching embodies teaching alive with spirit. Rather than pointing to some rarefied realm outside our ordinary lives, or a heightened dualism, the spirit is the great unifier of our disjointed personal and professional lives. When St. Paul speaks of the Spirit, following the traditions of his Israelite ancestors, he means that manifestation of God that gives us *integrity,* bringing outer and inner, heart and head, together—as well as unity with others. In the time of the Judges, like Deborah (Judg 4), the Spirit gave the *courage* to act in difficult circumstances; to the prophets the Spirit gave the *wisdom* of discernment between good and evil. The courage to act with integrity and wisdom qualifies as a prime virtue in the spiritual practice of teaching. To enliven teaching with the life of the spirit, we need to return to the actual sources within the tradition that can inform our spirituality with wisdom. One source, the monastic tradition, has often been mentioned but seldom plumbed. While the immediate "ancestor" of our present educational system is the university, our "grandparent" in the realm of educational endeavor is actually the monastery. The university has had an excellent record at developing knowledge and technique, but the monastic tradition of contemplative spirituality that preceded the university fostered wisdom.

This book arises out of my own experiences of disconnect between teaching and the spiritual life, one being pursued on my own time, and one in my professional life. My call to teach and my practice of teaching, in adult education in the Bowery of New York, in a middle school serving kids from the projects in North Carolina, and eventually in higher education, have seemed anything but contemplative. Too often work space became the denial of soul space, withholding parts of myself that were too precious or painful to incorporate, at the cost of wholeness. Too often the connection—a semiconductor linking these sparks—could not be made. Many of us may have survived by keeping a corner of ourselves, our inner lives, tucked away, inaccessible even to ourselves! Angry judgments, cynicism, an inner dialogue of negativity may litter that corner so that it is no longer an inner temple of repose. We have paid the price of disintegration and therefore dispiritedness. Yet those feelings, acknowledged and befriended, can open up places otherwise hidden in the whole interchange of the classroom.

Although my own arena of academic experience is higher education, and most of my examples will come from that realm, what I say applies to teaching at other levels: to the elementary and secondary levels, and even to the most essential teaching of all—to parenting. I write this at a point in my own career—over twenty years of postgraduate teaching—when I have withdrawn in order to discern the life-giving sources of my teaching. Despite having been a scholar nearly as long as I have been a teacher, I realize that mere scholarship will not save us. I have seen some of my colleagues shrivel up and die inwardly in the attempt to meet the competing demands of the profession, and I write this with them in mind.

A Crisis in Education

Articles describing the breakdown of education today abound; using words like *crisis, decline,* and *devaluation* in their titles, they depict a bleak and seemingly hopeless picture. Almost every educational publication appearing today offers different diagnoses of the problem. The U.S. Department of Education began its criticism of elementary and secondary education with *A Nation at Risk* in 1983. Soon after, publications on higher education singled out the "publish or perish mentality," with its subordination of teaching to research, as problematic. Some fault the faculty, with their "cynical careerism, excessive competition and intellectual fragmentation"; or their "mix of scholarly alienation in self-enclosed and often self-confirming academic discourses." For others, students are the problem. Peter Sacks blames Generation X's lack of a work ethic and lack of respect for education; William Willimon and Thomas Naylor point to substance abuse and indolence in the college generation. Others locate the problem in the educational climate's "general erosion of learning" and "drift into stagnation," in devalued diplomas and deteriorating standards; or in decreased government support, downsizing, or changes in college population, coupled with unsupported criticisms of faculties and their workloads. As one educator concludes, "The only point everyone seems to agree on is that we do, in fact, have a problem."[3] While all of the above analyses have merit, one must ask directly: Has the heart, which once pumped blood into the academic enterprise, gone out of the whole endeavor? The many articles pouring out of education journals suggest that we are at a stalemate, uncertain of our course or of the solution to the multiple problems diagnosed. Or, viewed differently, we are at a contemplative moment, a moment for inner searching. We can either capitalize on the fully contemplative nature of such a moment or dissipate it in a series of blind and futile actions. We have tried to resolve our various cultural crises by more *doing,* until doing has become a virtual paroxysm.

While the monumental problems of the system are critical, perhaps the real crisis comes when we stand in front of a group of students who do not care about the things we care about so deeply—our subjects, our classes, learning itself. This has become a personal crisis since I first began teaching as a volunteer in an adult education program in the Bowery of New York. Each week when I rode the subway from the New York University campus in Greenwich Village to

Houston Street, I found an extremely motivated group of adult learners. My class consisted of people working long hours at low wages who were studying in order to turn their lives around by taking the G.E.D. exam. That exam meant climbing out of a life of poverty and making it into the mainstream of society. What I remember most is the students' gratitude, demonstrated in their desire to learn, their perseverance, their unflagging motivation. These mothers, factory workers, and waitresses never gave up or needed prodding. One night a young black man accompanied me on the IRT to my stop in Greenwich Village. All along the way through the grimy underground of New York, he asked how I could do this without pay. I could only reply that I loved teaching and loved seeing the students learn. Those students inspired me to love, and that teaching experience became a paradigm for me of what good teaching can be.

A few years later, I found myself in a classroom of Vietnam veterans and Hispanics, almost all of them first generation college students, and again I felt their intense desire to learn, to grow, to absorb whatever I could give. One student in the class spoke up one day, "If we listen too closely to what you teach and the choices you lay before us, we may have to change our lives." These students had come from difficult lives and were ready not only for information but for transformation. They had already put their lives on the line in the streets or the battlefield, and found in the classroom another place for this courage and risk. In those moments I gained an understanding of how transformative teaching can be. Despite the continual wearing down, I resolved not to give up on the potential for transformation that teaching and learning can be.

Yet, we teachers seldom seem to offer them this transformation. "Objective" teaching and learning, the norm in most of our educational endeavors today, has sadly meant almost the direct opposite of transformation. We settle for an "instrumental rationality," a form of thinking and teaching that focuses on results, on tests, on success.[4] On the institutional level, this objectivism once meant a management-by-objectives approach. In the mid-1970s, I worked at a national laboratory for higher education whose goal was instructing administrators in this approach. Education, administrators felt, could be managed by a set of objectives. This MBO approach, like its counterparts today, from the administrative down to the classroom level, was designed to *prevent* the unexpected rather than to learn from it. After working as an editor of these management manuals for several years, I sought a job in a place that some would say occupied the other end of the career ladder for educators—teaching middle-school language arts. I have always considered this experience, teaching three totally different levels of eighth-grade language students, both my own boot-camp preparation—making everything else seem easy—and the place where I encountered the most dedicated "lifers" I have known. From them I learned to give the sixteen-year-old non-readers books about kids who like themselves lived in projects housing, and portfolios in which they could take pride and share with others in collaborative learning. Their desks were all askew, but brought students together in non-confrontational ways (until the principal insisted we go back to the "proper rows"). In this fairly disordered classroom, where the unexpected was the norm, I began to see real transformation.

This book rests on the premise that although we teachers cannot directly and immediately change some constituencies—government agencies, administrative bureaucracies, and students—we can change ourselves. Many voices from *outside* call for faculty to change, but little today promotes the interior searching and listening that facilitate true change. As Parker Palmer puts it: "The transformation of teaching must begin in the transformed heart of the teacher.

Only in the heart searched and transformed by truth will new teaching techniques and strategies for institutional change find sure grounding."[5] To renew education today means renewing our own hearts, and the contemplative path can lead us there.

Teaching as *Tradere Contemplativa*

The whole of the life of teaching and learning were once contemplative, to the degree that they involved a withdrawal from the burdens and activities of society for a time of sustained reflection. The Dominicans, founded in the twelfth century as a teaching order, take their motto from St. Thomas Aquinas, who said to teach is *tradere contemplativa* ("to share the fruits of contemplation"). The Dominican motto may sound ironic or absurd to us whose activity, pace, and workload have increased to record levels today. Yet, I still very much believe that teaching offers a way of life rich with possibilities for contemplation. I believe that in teaching we share not only the fruits, but the *practice* of contemplation with our students. Certainly, given the "sweat equity" of teaching, a contemplative view of it seems at least paradoxical, if not foolish. If we don't continue to achieve, numerous government reports and educational publications tell us, we will fall behind in our hypothetical education race. The pace of a curriculum (from *cursus,* meaning "running in rapid motion") literally has us running along to keep up. By definition, curriculum is not contemplative; it does not take the time to see into the temple that is in our midst. In the schools where I have taught, the pressure to bring students up to full intellectual maturity is so great that it usually entails teaching core courses overloaded with content and skills objectives. However, the most helpful comment I received in teaching these courses came from a colleague who told me, "Our task is not to cover the material but to uncover it." How in such situations do we uncover the material, that is, take the veils off and make it revelatory? A gesture of balance, such as contemplative teaching represents, is countercultural to say the least.

Paradoxically, seeing our teaching as contemplative means seeing that we already have everything we need. Such an awareness contradicts the striving, overzealous, achievement-oriented attitude we are trained in and then pass on to our students in one form or another. This statement, "You already have everything you need," speaks of grace, of presence, of a foundational, ontological, and ultimately transformative love. Most of us probably never heard this kind of affirmation in our training. If anything, we were told to do more, produce more, keep striving for perfection. We have been victims of the out-of-balance perfectionism of patriarchy.

Such an attitude of unconditional acceptance is actually a deeply contemplative one. If we were to say to our students, "You already have everything you need," we would deeply affirm each of them as a human being already carrying the image of God, already deeply known, accepted, and loved by God from the beginning. Although it seems a radical message for a teacher to send (even threatening to put her or him out of business if the student takes it too seriously), it may well reflect the message of both Christ and Socrates as teachers.[6] I believe that Jesus, too, was a contemplative teacher, a teacher whose deep acceptance of others taught them who they could be.

If the contemplative life comprises the roots of any endeavor, then the contemplative roots of our teaching must sink ever deeper into the ground of our hopes in order to bear fruit. Some of these grounds are psychological and personal, and the contemplative task requires us to search our hearts and our souls for the resources of faith, hope, and love that abide there. Some of them are archival without being archaic, so that we can still retrieve from them their wisdom and truth, making them again living traditions. We will open a conversation, then, with monks of the early Christian monastic tradition.

Monks and Teaching

Thomas Merton, in his essay "Learning to Live," makes a striking comparison between the monastery and the university. Merton boldly suggests that

> both monastery and university came into being in a civilization open to the sacred….they teach not so much by imparting information as by bringing the clerk (in the university) or the monk (in the monastery) to direct contact with "the beginning," the archetypal paradise world.[7]

We can imagine Merton as a student at Columbia University discovering this paradise of his own inner life. In a hidden way, studies laid the groundwork for his later contemplative life. Although he had great teachers like Dan Walsh, Merton's paradise did not reside in the "celestial store" of his teachers' ideas, theories, and abstractions. The gates to the archetypal paradise of restored relation to self, to others, and to God, lay within. Teaching returns to paradise insofar as it opens up this inner self, allowing the student as well as the teacher access to it; but it reinforces and confirms our exile from paradise as long as it remains outside the gate to the inner, truer self. Because we so seldom encounter this inner self in the classroom, the self of hopes and dreams and loves and delights, many seem to have accepted their exile from paradise.

The university is not a monastery, nor would we really want it to be. The distances between them in their beginnings and the divergences their paths have taken subsequently have become too great. We may seem far removed in our classrooms from the monk's peaceful, hermetic existence, but in one way we do not differ. When St. Anthony went out into the desert to seek God, he found himself instead in a life-and-death struggle with demonic temptations. The daily struggle with cynicism in our schools mirrors the monk's or hermit's battle with his own demons. St. Bernard of Clairvaux, a twelfth-century monk, named some of the demons that those who pursued knowledge had to face. We teachers can learn from him the true purpose of knowledge:

> For there are some who desire to know only for the sake of knowing; and this is disgraceful curiosity. And there are some who desire to know, that they may become known themselves; and this is disgraceful vanity....And there are also some who desire to know in order to sell their knowledge, as for money, or for degrees; and this is disgraceful commercialism. But there are also some who desire to know in order to edify; and this is love.[8]

Vanity, commercialism, credentials, even disinterested curiosity (though some might argue with this one), those are still the demons flying about our inner deserts. But they can be vanquished by love.

Lectio Divina and Teaching[9]

The monastic tradition sought wisdom through the practice of *lectio divina*, an especially rich resource for an intellectual life not content to be merely intellectual. As a modern Benedictine, Sr. Joan Chittister, has explained it: "*Lectio* is a slow, reflective process that takes us down below the preoccupations of the moment, the distractions of the day to that place where the soul holds the residue of life."[10] *Lectio divina,* as a method of reading sacred texts, seeks those underground streams of the spirit that well up into the life of the mind. As monks see it, *lectio divina* begins in simple reading or listening, but opens gradually into contemplation of divine mystery. The path is a path of heart that involves four stages:

- reading
- meditation
- prayer
- contemplation

This book on teaching and the contemplative life applies the four-fold design of *lectio divina*—reading, meditation, prayer, and contemplation—as metaphors for the practices of a contemplative teaching style. Each stage becomes a practice in the unfolding of a contemplative teaching style. Contemplative teaching calls on us to "read" by way of the heart, knowing not only objectively but also by *connection* to ourselves and to others. To paraphrase Kathleen Norris, the "cloister walk" runs right through our ordinary lives and world, even through our classrooms. The classroom's "cloister walk" leads through the monks' practices of *lectio divina,* beginning with simple reading.

We may well question the appropriateness of applying a method of sacred reading to texts other than sacred Scripture. When there is "nothing sacred," texts are just verbiage in what some have called the "hollow curriculum,"[11] a curriculum with little reference to spirituality and religion. Yet, a method such as *lectio divina,* introduced into these profane contexts, can reverse this "no-saying" trend. *Lectio* can serve as a small weapon of the spirit in the struggle against students' boredom, disinterest, and lack of desire to read. The practice of *lectio divina* can enable the objective to become subjective and thereby transformative, to enter our being and become part of us, without losing its objective status. In choosing *lectio divina* as a template for teaching and learning, I mean to be as "non-invasive" as possible, not to suggest *how* anyone might teach their subject or class, but merely to hint at the spiritual dimension that is possible.

Corresponding to *lectio* (reading) is **attention,** an abiding energy of the mind that is a just and loving gaze upon reality; corresponding to *meditatio* is **reflection,** the turning over and mirroring from different angles of the subjects that we attend to; corresponding to *oratio* is prayer's **receptivity** and relatedness, that inner openness allowing us to be moved and changed by what we attend to and reflect upon, making transformation possible; and finally *contemplatio,* which meant seeing God, leads to that **transformative vision** that can see "that of God" in the other and in creation. This ladder of reading, meditation, prayer, and contemplation integrates the senses, intellect, heart, and intuitive vision, in effect the whole person, making possible the continual deepening that transformation involves:

- reading——attention
- meditation—reflection
- prayer—receptivity
- contemplation—transformation

In the next chapter, I lay out a groundwork of the history of spirituality surrounding the practices of *lectio divina.* The people we will meet in that chapter—St. Benedict, Guigo the Carthusian, and St. Thomas Aquinas—have all practiced contemplation. They teach us the instruments of *lectio divina* to bring us to the depths, to place us in more authentic relationship with the world and with others, and to leave us open to the transformative power of the Spirit. They introduce us to teaching as spiritual practice.

CHAPTER 1

Contemplation and Teaching

My Beloved, the mountains
The solitary, wooded valleys
The strange islands,
The sonorous rivers,
The whisper of the amorous breezes,
The tranquil night,
At the time of the rising of the dawn,
The silent music,
The sounding solitude,
The supper that recreates and enkindles love.
—St. John of the Cross, *Spiritual Canticle*[1]

What Is Contemplation?

Contemplation is an old term for an old practice that is ever new. What used to be called contemplation and the contemplative life is usually referred to as spirituality today, so that by using the old word, we root our language more deeply in the traditions that gave rise to it. Contemplative seeing could be described as loving what is, letting *what is* unfold its levels of meaning before us, and seeing with the "eyes of the heart."[2] By connecting us to the other in a more loving way than the selfish relationships of desire and use, it lets the other—whether the natural world, the person, or God—be other, and even rejoices in that otherness. We desperately need this nonutilitarian and nonimperialist attitude to counter the rampant consumerism of our time. The contemplative gaze is like that of the grandmother—bemused, delighted, sometimes saddened, but willing to let *be* this little person unfolding before her. Such a gaze must be like God's.

We can understand much about the nature of contemplation in the West simply by noting the etymology of the word. The Latin word *templum* has a nice ambiguity, referring both to the space in the sky or the earth set off for reading omens, or to a *tempus* or segment of time. Contemplation meant seeing into the temple and using its template to see sanctified space everywhere. A paradigm experience of contemplation is that of Isaiah of Jerusalem: "In the year that King Uzziah died, I saw the Lord sitting on a throne, high and lofty; the hem of his robe filled the temple" (Isa 6:1). Not only does Isaiah see the Lord, but he hears the angels proclaim, "The whole earth is full of his glory" (Isa 6:3). Contemplation implies a metaphor of seeing, first into the sacred space of the temple, and then into the whole world filled with God's glory. If the first moment, the Temple vision, is the moment of *theologia* (seeing God directly), the second moment, the glory of God filling the world, is the more contemplative *theoria* (literally "contemplation," seeing the world in God). A natural world seen *in God* is a sacred one.

I feel fortunate that at least during one period of my life I was drawn to the contemplative life, for it is in essence a life of peace and joy. In my freshman year of high school, a friend persuaded me to join a religious organization, where I learned the daily disciplines of *lectio divina* (we called it "spiritual reading") and contemplative prayer (we called it "mental prayer"). Although my friend left this group after a year, I remained and continued these practices until they led me into a more formally structured life in a contemplative religious community. Those contemplative practices left a deeper impact on me than anything I learned during years of schooling. Yet, I came to realize that in order to fulfill the contemplative vocation, I must live it in the world. I resolved to be a contemplative within my everyday life.

In the Middle Ages, within the external buttresses of monasteries and cathedrals and on pilgrimages, literally and figuratively, people found a way to the wholeness fragmented by the demands and frustrations of dailiness. Today, the external buttresses may have collapsed for many, but the call and challenge, along with the longing and loneliness, remain. Since Vatican II, and with the introduction of Eastern mysticism in the West, the understanding and practice of contemplation have become more inclusive. Both lay people and clergy, given sacred space and sacred time, can renew themselves as they renew their commitment to God.

If we find the concept of contemplation difficult to grasp today, it may be because as a culture we are not very contemplative any more. For most of us, our time-saving, labor-saving devices have not opened up sacred time but simply more entertainment and its correlative boredom, diminishing the openings to do things contemplatively, to "do what we are doing," as the medieval monks used to say. We either rush ahead, planning our next move, or mull over something past and usually regrettable. Washing dishes, doing laundry, growing our own food—even reading a good book—were once contemplative acts. As machines take over more and more, we remake ourselves in their image, unintentionally imitating and competing with them. Liturgically, a contemplative spirituality resembles the season of Advent, where we wait in darkness, expectantly, longingly, anxiously, waiting for birth. The darkness teaches us that there is much we do not see, do not control. The waiting and dark mask the inner growth toward the light. Yet, just as this season of Advent is dissipating today into the all-consuming Christmas rush, so our Advent experiences of contemplative living have been dissipating into the rush of instant gratification.

Contemplative Teaching

Yet, what does contemplation have to do with teaching? Much of what we do seems so worried and hurried, so scattered and at best merely task-fulfilling. *Contemplative* is probably the last adjective we would apply to the flurry of committee assignments, politicking in and out of departments, tenure pressures on both sides of that great divide, and so much else that occupies and preoccupies us as teachers. When one turns to the classroom—presumably a haven of the unharried search for truth and meaning and a place to hand down the valued traditions of our disciplines and crafts—one finds a microcosm of the system of rewards and punishments, mirroring the external world's ambition and one-upmanship. Recent articles speak to the intense pressures felt by students and teachers at all grade levels who are forced to give and pass standardized achievement tests.[3] Accompanying students' anxiety is teachers' fear of "dumbing-down" their subjects to get students to pass these tests. Institutional pressures seem like tidal waves at times, engulfing and destroying everything in their path, including those lone individuals who would seek to stem the tide.

In an academic world characterized by increasing discord, alienation, faculty burnout, student consumerism, and an overall market mentality, where does one find the temple of renewal? Whatever moves us toward our own transformation, even here in this messy world of compromises, is the "house of God" in our midst. Jacob, limp but transformed, is also the modern contemplative's prototype in his wrestling match with

God. As the Buddhists say, "nirvana is samsara," the bliss of transformation is right here in the cycle of birth and death, pain and glory. If contemplation has traditionally meant seeing the world as it really is, as sacred, we might say that contemplative teaching makes it possible to see sacred space or sacred time in and through the classroom. Given the academic world's frustrated expectations, resistance, boredom, and the students' need for entertainment, sacredness might be the last characteristic we would ascribe to the atmosphere.

In an ever more plugged-in, tuned-out culture, silence and slow time hint at what contemplation can bring to teaching and learning.[4] For the past few years, a group of faculty has been meeting weekly for an hour of Centering Prayer. We begin and end the hour with a few minutes of Gregorian chant, and in between concentrate on our breath or on a mantra. The hour acts as a pivot of peacefulness for the week, gently withdrawing our attention from the next task and onto a more pure form of the present moment. In an American society so bent on action, Taoism's *wu wei* ("doing without doing") and the New Testament's *kenosis* (self-emptying) have lessons to teach us. *Wu Wei*, "doing without doing," waiting for the effective action to emerge—waiting for holy power—has its counterpart in the biblical concept of *kenosis*, Christ's self-emptying. Whenever I have found myself practicing the stepping back and "not forcing" of Taoism's *wu wei*, or the emptying of *kenosis*, not trying to make things come out my way, fruitfulness follows.

One story unfortunately typifies the problem of "doing without doing." Teachers who undergo peer reviews report that when other teachers come into their classrooms and see students in small group discussions, or writing in journals, or some other form of quiet activity that looks like "doing nothing," teachers tell them they will come back when "something is happening" (i.e., a lecturing mode with the teacher dispensing information). Teacher performance and evaluation are on the line in the choice of a more contemplative mode. In a culture where being harried and pressured serves as the norm (and even first-graders feel stressed by the amount of homework they have), such a style may seem absurd, but it is the very antidote we need. If this antidote seems like one more thing to add to our already overbooked days, it might help to see it as doing what we are already doing with more of ourselves present. Although we fear it, that "nothing" may be the seedbed of new possibilities. An *ethic of presence* may be our best practice and the greatest gift we can offer our students. The Trappist monk Thomas Merton has put the case for us moderns to hear:

> Duty of the contemplative life....To provide an area, a space of liberty, of silence, in which possibilities are allowed to surface and new choices—beyond routine choice—become manifest. To create a new experience of time, not as stoppage, stillness, but as *"temps vierge"*— not a blank to be filled or an untouched space to be conquered and violated, but to enjoy its own potentialities and hopes and its own presence to itself. One's *own* time (not dominated by one's ego and its demands), hence open to others—*compassionate* time.[5]

For Thomas Merton, the contemplative life frees up an interior space from self-consciousness and plans, opening it to others, making it in effect a compassionate time. Contemplation is about making time our own and then giving it away.

Contemplation and the Christian Tradition of *Lectio Divina*

Within the Christian tradition, Thomas Aquinas has defined contemplation as a connection to the other that begins and ends in love. When we contemplatively know something or someone, we abide in them without judgment—we love. We can think of the term *contemplation* as simply the longing for that which is trying to be born in us, the longing to be real, to be connected, and to be in Love. It is that depth of ourselves that we suppress in the vain attempt to find "reality" and "connection" wholly outside ourselves. If Isaiah in his Temple vision is the archetypal Hebrew contemplative (Isa 6:1–13), so also is Jacob in his discovery that the "house of God," Bethel, is everywhere (Gen 28:10–17). As this latter example implies, contemplative seeing does not remain in the Temple or in the depths of self. It moves one out into the world, sanctified by the vision. To live the contemplative life has always meant seeking and seeing the sacred in the ordinary—not only seeing it but entering into it. While contemplation involves a moment of seeing, it embodies *practices* that enable and embody that seeing, and is therefore eminently practical. Contemplation, the practice of "revolutionary patience," as the monk Fr. Basil Pennington calls it, brings a transforming vision and energy to life's demands.

Because it embodies a way of love rather than of possession, of being rather than having, a way of union rather than domination or fusion, contemplation comprises a deeply religious way of being in the world. Just as it releases the loved object from possession, it releases the lover from possessiveness. Every lover knows this detachment, and every artist too. In contrast to linear, rational thought, in contemplative knowing the mind no longer actively organizes reality but is deeply content to *be* in it. Seeing contemplatively means in the most ordinary sense dissolving our usual cognitive frames on reality, delighting in what appears, and giving it deep assent.

Though the Eastern traditions of mysticism have taught us much about contemplation, we need not go outside the Christian tradition to find a contemplative way of life. We can locate contemplative themes in a Western tradition with a long and rich history, one that yields sources already well-rooted and suited to our soil. Three teachers who are themselves contemplatives can help us in our quest: St. Benedict of Nursia, Guigo the Carthusian, and St. Thomas Aquinas. Benedict founded the contemplative Western monastic life as we know it today; Guigo belonged to a monastic community that practiced a solitary life of contemplation; and Aquinas came from the emerging School tradition at the University of Paris where he taught that teaching *is* contemplative, that it is *tradere contemplativa:* sharing the fruits of contemplation.

St. Benedict of Nursia

St. Benedict of Nursia, our first interpreter of the contemplative life, was born about 480 in a region northeast of Rome. While in school at Rome, he became so scandalized by the hedonistic lifestyle of the other students that he left school and settled in a cave among the hills at Subiaco in Italy.[6] Monks found him there and begged him to become their teacher in the ways of God, so that even in solitude he began becoming a "teacher of the soul" and an "abba," or spiritual father. Although he warned them that his way would seriously disturb their lifestyle, the very monks who persuaded him to leave his solitary cave found his spiritual guidance so intolerable that they conspired to poison him! Every teacher can understand Gregory's understatement that they "found it hard to let go of what they had thought about with their old minds in order to ponder new things."[7] Yet, Benedict's first failure at being a teacher of the soul, along with the hardened resistance of his students, taught him to be wiser and more compassionate, in fact to be a real "teacher of the soul." Failure and resistance were *his* teachers.

Benedict learned a great lesson as well from another teacher, his twin sister, Scholastica.[8] In a famous incident, she provided the necessary counterpart to Benedict's sometimes fanatical adherence to rules. On one of their yearly visits, when the brother and sister met to speak of God and to pray together, as night came on, Benedict, bound more to *chronos* (clock) time than to the *kairos* of the "fullness of time," prepared to go home. His sister begged him to stay and continue speaking of heaven. Just as she began shedding abundant tears, the heavens opened in a torrential rain. Despite this climatic confirmation of Scholastica's tearful prayer, Benedict was at first shocked at her disobedience (even though he was her twin brother and not her father). Yet, the story, with its miraculous rain, seems to sanction the authority of *her wisdom* over Benedict's patriarchal model of authority. Indeed, Benedict's *Rule* might not be so justly famous for its moderation if it were not for the flexibility he learned from his sister. His *Rule* went on to establish "a school for God's service,"[9] where "nothing harsh or burdensome" but only a "little strictness" would be needed to expand the heart and amend faults.[10] This "Rule" allowed for both structure and freedom.

In his *Rule*, Benedict prescribed daily periods of *lectio divina,* sacred reading of scriptural texts. Both the more individual *lectio divina* and the communal *Opus Dei* (the Divine Office or Liturgy of the Hours) were Benedict's response to Paul's charge to "pray without ceasing" (1 Thess 5:17). *Lectio divina* became not simply spiritual reading of the Bible, but a "practice of mindfulness to the presence of God in the Word" and therefore a prayerful response to the whole of life.[11] The ordinary page of Scripture was the monk's *templum,* and by delving into it he (or she) would find God. With the simple introduction of this practice, Benedict opened a pathway to the whole life of contemplation. Contemporary Cistercians, who also follow the Benedictine Rule, define *lectio divina* as "reverential listening." Changing the verb from reading to listening makes it a response of reverence to the whole of life. The listening quality of lectio (what Benedict called praying "with the ears of the heart") entails reverencing the word in all the ways the Word, God's self-expression, manifests itself—in the earth, in human beings, and in being itself. This process over time allows the text of Scripture to descend from the head to the heart, to embed its meaning in the being and life of the monk so that it can become enfleshed there.

For these early monks, reading became a technology of the spirit, part of a toolkit for contemplation. Reading was rhythmic; the monk would read a verse of Scripture, then "sit" with it, pausing to reflect or pray spontaneously. He would resume reading until another word, phrase, or line would kindle the heart and imagination. The poet Rainer Maria Rilke gives a description of a person practicing the rhythm of *lectio divina* in a more secular context: "He does not always remain bent over his pages; he often leans back and closes his eyes over a line he has been reading again, and its meaning spreads through his blood."[12] *Lectio divina* is the kind of reading that frustrates the urge to get through, to get anything, but instead places the reader in slow time, where all the moves are God's. A person doing sacred reading has to resolve to waste time, a terribly countercultural, counterproductive move in this media- and Web-saturated culture.

During a needed respite from the intensity of graduate school one summer, I visited the Benedictine monastery at St. John's Abbey as a guest of the Abbey. I played tennis, swam in the lake, took long walks, used the library for study, and joined the monks three times a day for the Liturgy of the Hours as well as for Mass. Even in such a brief stay as mine, there was balance between work and play and prayer, suspending for a while the obsessive round of study of my life as a graduate student. I found, in the Benedictine lifestyle, time for prayer, work, study, and play, and that they are all somehow influential, all flowing into one another.

What we teachers can take from Benedict is a sense of *balance* between the contemplative and active sides of our teaching and a willingness to construct a spiritual "rule" for our life. Just as Benedict learned from his sister, and from his first failures as a teacher of the soul, in our lives we need "nothing harsh or oppressive" but the steadiness of a balanced life, one in which work becomes prayer. The Latin root of the word for *rule* ("trellis") suggests a frame where a plant can grow toward the light in its own way, but guided by a structure, a practice.[13] The practices of *lectio divina* applied to teaching can become just such a trellis for us and our students. Like a trellis, they offer the gentle guidance of a structured practice, while leaving open many possibilities for growth.

Guigo the Carthusian's Ladder of Monks

Benedict's practice of *lectio divina* was extended into four stages or practices several centuries later by another medieval monastic order, the Carthusians. Like Benedict, Bruno, the founder of the Carthusians, started in a school that scandalized him. Unlike Benedict, however, Bruno not only completed his course of study at the cathedral school of Reims, France, but went on to become a "doctor" of the cathedral canon as well as its rector.[14] Yet, the call to a life given to God alone proved stronger than his career ambitions. With six companions, Bruno entered the remote valley of the Chartreuse, nestled in the mountains of France, and built there a series of hermitages that were to become the foundation of the Carthusian Order.

Carthusians follow the Benedictine Rule, but their statutes emphasize the teaching role of their cell, which actually consists of a fairly spacious two-story structure surrounded by a garden. To those of us who crave solitude such a place sounds ideal, but any cell, even any dormitory room, can become a teacher with plenty of lessons to teach! Discipline or boredom, addiction or freedom, depression and anxiety or hope—these are its continual lessons and choices. From the beginning, the Carthusian motto was "God, and God alone, in solitude,"[15] but Carthusians saw their solitude as bringing them closer to others, paradoxically uniting them in an intimate love.[16] Solitude's wrestling match with our inner demons of boredom and restlessness (what monks called *acedia*) can become impossible to win, unless the Spirit enables us to overcome them. With the cell or the Spirit as teachers, the Carthusians continued to thrive century after century. In the late twelfth century, one of these Carthusians, Guigo II, the ninth prior of the Grande Chartreuse, wrote a letter to another monk which included a treatise on prayer called the *Ladder of Monks*.[17] That treatise holds the key to the four practices of *lectio divina*.

The *Ladder of Monks* employs the metaphor of the ladder to lay out four stages or "rungs" of the contemplative life, from reading Scripture, to meditation, to prayer, and finally contemplation. The third-century theologian, Origen, had used this image to explore three stages of ascent to God in prayer: *purgation* for beginners; *illumination* for proficients; and *union* for the perfect. This analogy became so standard throughout the history of spirituality that Guigo adopted it, adding an extra rung for his four-step process of *lectio, meditatio, oratio,* and *contemplatio*.

Guigo's *Ladder of Monks* begins on the bottom rung with the Benedictine *lectio divina* ("sacred reading"), which takes the words of Scripture to heart by repeating them over and over. It moves up the ladder to *meditatio*, meditation or rumination on the words which seeks their inner meaning; then to *oratio*, the prayer that engages the heart in response to God's leading; and finally, to *contemplatio*, contemplation which Guigo describes as the point where "the mind is in some sort lifted up to God and held above itself." Thus, reading is for beginners, meditation for the proficient, prayer for the perfect, and contemplation for those in heaven.

In adopting Guigo's ladder as our paradigm for a contemplative way of teaching, we may need to dismantle it at the same time. The metaphor of the ladder with its implication of an ascent from earth to heaven worked well in Guigo's dualistic, two-story universe. While Guigo meant the ladder image to convey spiritual ascent, for us moderns it can also tap into our competitive climbing and achievement instincts, and thereby defeat the purpose of any spiritual growth. In short, it can lead to pride, which only replaces material striving with spiritual striving.

A more pervasive, and this-worldly, image encountered today is the spiritual journey. With the notion of the spiritual journey we suggest walking rather than climbing, and at least are back on the ground, landing on our feet in a more grounded, this-worldly context. Yet, even our walking involves trying to get somewhere, rather than simply to *practice* each of these stages. With the concept of practice, the metaphors of *circle* and *play* may prove more helpful than the ladder's climbing or the journey's linear walking. Each stage is present to and within the others like interdependent parts of a mandala or a circle dance. If we see each aspect of *lectio divina* at the corners of a mandala, they can all point us to the center, the sacred. We can invert Guigo's ladder metaphor to one of descent and deepening, or we can bend it to form a never-ending circle. The journey of contemplation is not so much a straightforward journey, charted in stages of "progress," but a spiraling round the Center of one's own being and life. In the view of a contemporary Carthusian, the ladder of *lectio divina* is a "journey towards the heart." I find it tremendously bracing that even if I might be making the same old mistakes in practice, I am in a different place, and indeed, have become a different person.

Maria Harris's wonderful little book, *Women and Teaching*, proposes the metaphor of the dance for the series of steps involved in teaching. The steps in the dance can go "backward or forward, can incorporate one another, can involve turn and re-turn, can move down as well as up, out as well as in, and be sometimes partnered, sometimes solitary."[18]

Guigo's "ladder," then, is an *intuitive* one, the destiny of which is the heart's intimacy and openness to and with all. He gives all of us who are students of life a fourfold way of opening up to life and reality at ever greater levels of depth, relatedness, and receptivity to the sacred. From Guigo and his religious order we teachers can take the "journey towards the heart."

St. Thomas Aquinas and Play

While Benedict and Guigo exemplify the monastic tradition of spirituality, St. Thomas Aquinas represents the scholastic tradition of university studies. Living a scant century after Guigo, he occupies a wholly different spiritual and intellectual universe, the world of the university. Unlike Benedict and Guigo, Thomas was not driven from his studies by scandals but studied arduously in Cologne and taught at the great new university of Paris. If Benedict and Guigo defined the contemplative life by living it, Thomas defined it in his theology and explicitly linked it to the life of teaching. As a teacher, philosopher, and theologian, and someone who dedicated his life to God, Thomas integrated the life of the spirit with the life of the mind. In fact, he could accept no real dichotomy between them.

For the Dominicans, the Order of Preachers and teachers of whom St. Thomas Aquinas (1225–1274) is the outstanding exemplar, teaching was primarily a call to the contemplative life. This call found completion in the vocation to "share with others the fruits of contemplation" *(tradere contempla-*

tiva), the very nature of teaching. Thomas describes this twofold call with the imagery of light: "It is better to illumine [to bring this light to others] than merely to shine."[19] The best teachers are those whose light is reflective, lighting up their students so their lights can shine. As teachers reflect a light greater than their own—from countless forebears who have illuminated them, and from the Holy Spirit—they mirror that light to their students.

It helps to remember at the outset that the purpose of teaching as spiritual practice is to maximize joy. Thomas' special contribution to a reflection on contemplation is the note of joy. Paradoxically, Thomas Aquinas, that most hard-working of all intellectuals, characterizes contemplation primarily in terms of *play.* For Thomas, contemplation involves the kind of "graceful playfulness" discovered in true friendship and in love. In play we get to be both rule-conscious and playful, letting loose of our ordinary tunnel vision. The usually sober Thomas speaks of the delights of contemplation. In contemplation we experience delight first because we realize our own "intellectual" nature. Thomas' use of the word *intellect* is closer to what we refer to as *intuition.* Contemplative learning delights us further because we contemplate what we love and thereby increase our love for it.[20] Thomas emphasizes the contemplative delight both of inhabiting our own nature and of connecting with others as they are. For Thomas Aquinas, we are most contemplative when we are lovers! Today, the idea that in teaching we begin and end with what we love has perhaps not fully recovered from an Enlightenment suspicion. The Enlightenment period, so captivated by reason and objectivity and so fearful of love, distrusted "the heart's reasons" as too subjective and emotional. For many educators today, love still seems a bit too "interested," too passionate.

Thomas makes a helpful distinction between two objects of the contemplative life. The principal object is the divine itself; the secondary object, "God's effects."[21] We could call these two types of contemplative knowing "mystical" and "incarnational." Mystical knowing seeks to know God directly *(theologia)*, while incarnational knowing seeks to know God through God's traces in creation *(theoria)*. From Thomas Aquinas, the clear-eyed scholastic philosopher and systematic theologian, we teachers can take the joy of playing with God's traces in the world. Teachers and scholars engage more often than not in this incarnational form of contemplative knowing whether we realize it or not. We cannot encounter divine truth, the first type of contemplation, directly—for we do not see "face to face," but only "through a glass darkly" (1 Cor 13:12). However, when we know God's "effects" or "traces," the "tracks" God has left in the world, we become contemplative knowers and lovers, knowing what we are made to know. Teaching then can become "graceful playfulness." We can learn from Thomas that our true nature is contemplative, so that in teaching and learning contemplatively, we—students *and* teachers—become who we truly are. Because contemplation both connects us to our own true selves and relates us to others in love, it brings delight, an experience which teachers too seldom allow themselves in the classroom. We may not make room for joy.

Spiritual Practice: Depth, Relatedness, and Transcendence

But how do we create a model of teaching that incorporates Thomas' joy, Guigo's contemplative journey of the heart, and Benedict's balance? Simply put, how do we make teaching a spiritual practice? In the remainder of this chapter, we connect teaching with the lessons and practices of contemplation. Benedict, Guigo, and Thomas can serve as guides in making teaching a spiritual practice. If Benedict and Guigo lead us to the depths of our hearts and beyond them to God, the *intuitive* contemplative dimensions, Thomas' spirituality connects us in love to the world around us, the *cosmological* contemplative dimension.

Those who disparage practice (and I am one of them when I think back to my days sitting on the piano bench) might do well to remember that we are embodied beings, whose inner selves seek expression in action. I would like to rescue a notion of practice as flowing from our inner being to the world. We need to give form to our good intentions. I *use* technology, but I cultivate practice. The word *technique,* for many, particularly in K–12, conjures up too many quick fixes that turn us away from our own inner voices and instincts. We need technique as "embodied grace."

Beginning any practice is as difficult as trying to water a dry garden with buckets of water, as St. Teresa of Avila (1515–1582) says about beginning the practice of prayer. At first, the water comes from a distance only through laborious human effort. Later, water simply wells up directly from the spring and begins to overflow without any human skill.[22] Teresa's analogy is especially appropriate since it concerns deepening levels of meditation, involving a deeper connection to the inner life and to God. In many religious communities people simply ask, "What is your practice?" not "Have you been saved?" There is little of that *fait accompli* notion of completion. One group of teachers speaks of their daily practices in the simplest of terms: splashing cold water to honor the directions and the elements, reading a poem, pouring the warmth of a cup of coffee, lighting a candle to write, and to "honor the light, the life force, and to open to receive what may come."[23] These practices and rituals become the meeting place of meaning and manners, of vision and practicality. Over time, the work we set out to do in a practice shifts to other areas of our life. Settling on a group of practices—like yoga, meditation, journaling, or those of *lectio divina*—forces us to navigate the middle ground between accomplishment and failure. When we commit our-selves to them faithfully, practices make us constant learners, give expression to our hopes, and join us to others engaged in them, that is, to a community of practitioners. Practices in effect become our "Rule."

Teaching, an ancient art, embraces many practices. In rela-tion to the tradition of contemplation, teaching is paradoxi-cal practice; it encompasses Thomas Aquinas' "mixed life" of contemplation and action, a constant dialectical swing between doing and being. In teaching, sometimes the mind seems busy planning and deciding, and at other times it sim-ply waits, receiving ideas from many sources about what is going on in the classroom. In a polarized model of teaching, teacher as active, student as passive, it seems as if the waiting is all on one side—the student's side. But in a contemplative teaching style, the teacher learns to wait as the student finds voice and shares power. The spiritual practices of *lectio, med-itatio, oratio,* and *contemplatio*—translated into attention, reflection, receptivity, and transformation—belong to those who teach as well as to those who are being taught.

Contemporary culture may so eclipse our understanding of what it means to be religious—substituting the moralism of avoiding personal sin (where will predominates) or the gnosticism of private "spiritual" knowledge (where intellect may predominate) or the tribalism of denominational reli-gions (where club predominates)—that we need to outline some essential elements of spiritual practice to appreciate its merits. Spiritual practices are healthiest when they draw on religion's substantiality, its wisdom traditions, its "trellises" or structures for supporting and sustaining personal efforts, and its communities of correction and affirmation. We can identify at least three elements of spiritual practices that Benedict, Guigo, and all serious practitioners exemplify: (1) **psychological and spiritual depth:** self-knowledge; (2) **relat-edness:** acknowledging and strengthening relationship with others, including relationship to a tradition; and (3) **not-doing:** leaving ourselves really open to the working of the Spirit, to a transcendence that belies mere self-help.

Psychological and Spiritual Depth

Spiritual practices aim to connect us to the depth dimension of our acts, to the source of our choices. While morality emphasizes making active choices (and we Americans love this practicality and immediacy, like being prolife or antigay), the spiritual dimension opens up a background of fears, doubts, desires, and hopes—the messiness of the heart—that lies behind and sometimes subverts these choices. Not simply the act of adultery, an easy target for moralizers, but the more covert coveting in the heart constitutes the root of the problem, making the Bible's solution "radical," one that goes to the roots. Both Jesus and Paul give us a spirituality that directs us to the depths of the heart. Secular terminology calls it the unconscious; the Bible has always called it the heart. The Bible is full of this kind of messy ambiguity. The biblical writers point to these psychological and spiritual depths, because that is where God meets us.

In our Westerns, and in their contemporary incarnations such as *Star Wars,* we Americans celebrate the lonely hero whose choices in the moment of crisis are monumental ones. We love heroes. Spirituality and spiritual practice, on the other hand, point to the continual daily choices running in the background, "the quotidian mysteries," most of them mundane and unremarkable, that must constantly be reexamined in light of God's call. (Living every day with your spouse, caring for your child, going into class to face students each day, occur in "ordinary time.") Spirituality belongs to the recessive "ground," while the moral and heroic deeds and experiences constitute the outstanding "figure." People wandering in the background of the biblical drama, making undramatic choices, are its crucial players.[24] Often the "nobodies," peasant girls like Mary, fishermen like Peter, make all the difference by their unseen yes or no to God and to the other to whom they must respond.

Relatedness

While many people think of spirituality as emphasizing exclusively the relationship to God, as if God would allow such limitation, the mystics experienced *greater* relationship with others because of their intense love for God. Although the depth of knowledge of self may tear us away from the herd, at least for a time, true spiritual endeavor always returns us to others. The Spirit does not always call us to a set of deeds and hurdles or to an esoteric knowledge, but to the harder realities of relationship, and in this the Bible differs from the heroic epics and treatises of the Greeks. Because they reduce our self-importance or ego, spiritual practices convey a realization of interconnectedness. They involve the self-correction of connections to a wisdom tradition. The depth dimension of honesty and courage in relationship to God, of turning one's real face to God, undergirds real relationship to others. If contemplation is seeing what is really there, then it more deeply relates us to the world, not to our own fancies and projections. Practices of *lectio* help us get beneath our intellectual defenses. This way of engaging reality has more to do with awe than with critique, with humility than with mastery.

Not-doing and Transcendence

As many contemporary spiritual writers have said, we are not human doings but human beings, and we do not draw our fundamental self-worth from achievement but from an innate goodness called in the Christian tradition the "image of God." Unlike sheer moral endeavor, which emphasizes doing, spiritual practices involve the *not-doing* of just being. Our "practice" may seem to us more like doing nothing, though it is essentially "waiting for God." The very depth of a spiritual practice paradoxically promises a transcendence that does not always happen when we are in control, being self-righteously moral. The Spirit calls one into periods of intentional rest from activity, into Sabbath.

Teaching as Spiritual Practice

Teaching may seem an unlikely form to express all three elements of spiritual practice: psychological and spiritual depth, relatedness, and not-doing. Yet teaching has the potential to become spiritual practice when we encounter within our own depths our fears and desires, our real relation to our students and subjects, and the sacred in and among us. Teaching is profoundly relational, even at first glance. But its capacity to engage the "vertical" dimensions of depth and transcendence has barely been plumbed. Even in the relational aspect of the life of teaching, we touch upon sacred mystery. When our students offer, from their own sacred inner space, their tentative, provisional attempts to write or speak, they give us a sacrament of their own mystery. Indeed, we create sacred time, a kind of Sabbath of renewal, when we take time to honor their offerings.

But a contemplative point of view even looks at the mundane space of the classroom as sacred ground. Of course, the idea that we can find sacred space anywhere depends on a thoroughly incarnational theology. This theology proclaims that the Word, Christ, became flesh and entered the world, making it holy, and that God is with us.

Teaching as Lectio: *Reading Our Students, Our Subjects, Ourselves*

To uncover the depth, relationality, and transcendence of our vocation, we need a sacred reading, a *lectio divina,* of our very vocation. The sacredness of *lectio divina* consists in an adverbial quality, an attitude, with which we approach any text or encounter to have it teach us and to be changed by it. *Lectio divina,* then, is the practice of reverence. Reading, *lectio,* is a metaphor for ever-deepening encounter with the "text" of our own depths, of students, and of God. Contemplative teaching attempts to "read" the sacred and mysterious ground of communion with ourselves, our students, and the sacred itself.

Reading Students

Some of the reading required of us as teachers entails "reading" our students and their lives. What if we were to see our students as possessing a story that we need to read, even in classes that do not remotely involve the use of autobiography? What if their stories were as real to us as the subjects we teach, though both we and they may never know their stories in full? Then our teaching would become a *lectio divina,* a sacred reading of the stories in our students. Parker Palmer, who spent a year at the college where I taught, noted that we were very good at telling *our* story, "the myth of the college," but not very good at eliciting the stories of those—teachers and students—who came there to learn and to teach.[25]

Students from African-American or Latino homes, or from Asia or Africa, can come to college and for four years not have the chance to tell their stories; they may even be made to forget them in order to learn the bigger story. As one of my students from Peru said to me recently, "If I were to go back home, you would not see anything of this 'me' there. I am a different person there than here. Because of my lifestyle, I would not even look like a student to you there." What are these stories that so completely elude us, and how can we help students integrate them into their own learning so that they do not learn to be schizoid?

Thomas Merton said it well: "The purpose of education is to show a person how to define himself authentically and spontaneously in relation to the world—not to impose a pre-fabricated definition of the world. Still less an arbitrary definition of the individual himself."[26] We need to enable students to read themselves if they are to achieve the real goal of contemplative learning: learning who is the "I" who learns. Many "arbitrary definitions," or social constructions as we say today, offer to supplant the "I" who speaks. It is difficult to find the psychological and spiritual depths of self when that self has disappeared. Having learned to dissolve my own "I" in graduate school, I still unconsciously pass that unselving on to my students.

Often our schools serve as training-grounds in inauthenticity and duplicity, becoming what Paulo Freire calls a "necrophilic" education,[27] an exercise in death of soul. While students learn *dead* letters, they also learn how *not* to be themselves. When education itself conspires to sink the person further into the collective, to enable escape from the true self, one wonders whether it is education at all. In a realm of competition (and its flip side, fear), students *learn* how to more cleverly fake it: looking engaged when they feel bored, getting by, by doing little. As the "I" of students' stories, feelings, and beliefs dissolves into the impersonal and passive voice of "academese," *they* feel they have arrived. The danger is that when authenticity becomes the norm, students will become experts at faking even that authenticity!

Sincerity in a situation that nearly compels duplicity— looking for good grades while hiding one's discontent and malaise on the one hand, looking for good evaluations while hiding cynicism on the other—begins to look impossible. Few would repudiate Socrates' ideal of knowing thyself, but just as few would follow him into the "therapy of soul" that he counseled as the essence of education. If education still means "leading out of," will we only draw out a collection of false masks from the students? But students know better than their elders, perhaps, the pain of living a lie. They do not have as much practice at dulling that pain and hiding the true self. The pain in their young lives—the woundedness of broken families, of abuse, of being born into a world of enormous suffering—can prove the means, some would say *grace,* of awakening them and us to authenticity. When we teachers take the risk of allowing our teaching to become contemplative—of stopping, listening, and really seeing in our classrooms—and of facing the pain and confusion in ourselves and in our students, we allow our students to open to the possibility of genuine understanding and, therefore, of genuine transformation.

We create what Margaret Wheatley has called an "open system," one that draws energy from its environment rather than losing energy in entropy.[28] Drawing on the work of contemporary physicists in her study of self-organizing systems in organization, she found that some form of *disequilibrium* is actually needed for the growth of the system as a whole and for the persons in them. Each element of a contemplative teaching style attempts to respond to the environment by way of opening rather than merely by self-defined, predetermined "disciplines." In our opening to students and subjects, what if we envisioned our "fields" (the areas we survey, track, and use our disciplines to traverse) as making room for students as part of the treasure waiting to be discovered out there? Our students' stories—their personal, inviolable reality—open the "system" of the school's institutional structure to the environment. My task as a contemplative teacher is to "read" at least some aspect of students' internal story and help them connect it to the larger story we are telling.

Each time I begin teaching a new class, even in a subject I have taught before, I learn where my students are along the whole spectrum of belief and disbelief, resistance and acceptance. The dislocation they already feel in coming to college is compounded by new and sometimes more fundamental dislocations. These dislocations, not only in their study of religion but in science, philosophy, history, and political science, often go unacknowledged. My job becomes learning how to accompany them on this journey, to be with them in this new uncomfortable place, that is, to educate ("lead them out") into relationship with this subject so that they can return home again. Sometimes I fail the class, figuratively and literally. I fail to take in the true nature of the students before me, to experience my teaching "ever anew from the other side." In his classic essay on education, Jewish philosopher Martin Buber says of the teacher:

> Without the action of his spirit being in any way weakened he must at the same time be over there, on the surface of that other spirit which is being acted upon—and not of some conceptual, contrived spirit, but all the time the wholly concrete spirit of this individual and unique being who is living and confronting him.[29]

Teachers must experience their own teaching "ever anew from the other side," as Martin Buber puts it. Teacher becomes learner in the give and take of the classroom, as students upset and break through even the teacher's tightly packaged worldview. As an Anglo facing whole classes of Hispanic students, as a white woman standing before African-American students, as a member of the privileged middle class with students from Appalachia who know poverty first-hand, and as a liberal Catholic, I learn that my categories and assumptions, and those of our textbooks, may need to open up to include the experiences and knowledge of the students before me.

Reading Our Subjects

How do we read our subjects together with our students so that the depths open up between subject and student? As long as we keep knowledge outside, continue to exchange it on tests and papers, like so much currency, we cannot entirely avoid its commodification. The banking method of teaching where the teacher *deposits* facts, ideas, and theories into the student's brain and the student regurgitates them on tests, becomes appropriate in contexts where students are referred to as "customers" or "consumers."[30] The banking method employs not *communion* but consumption. Further, it reinforces the consumer ethic in our students, goading them into becoming consumers in the marketplace of knowledge. Contemplation does not consume, and thus thwarts this ethic of consumerism in our culture. In order to bring a more contemplative style of teaching to these places, we must first expel the "money changers" from the inner sanctum of intellectual and spiritual growth.

Discovering the mysterious ground of communion between our students and subjects is a sacred feast, a holy communion. Yet, in our classrooms today, there is much famine. Despite the abundant fare available in the supermarkets of ideas, as much cognitive as real anorexia exists (as well as the bulimia of cramming and spitting up on exams), so that even knowledge consumption is down. Knowledge is no longer nurture; as our students sense this, they become less willing to partake.

Without the encounter between the subjectivity of our students and what they objectively learn, they lose the chance to do the greatest learning of all: the learning to be who they

really are. So at one and the same time I ask students for a
kenosis, an emptying of their conventional thinking—to
leave their homeland for a while—and to explore it in relationship to themselves, to return home. I ask for the *depth*
and *relatedness* that constitute two elements of a spiritual
practice. Reading Galileo or Isaac Newton or the texts of a
sixteenth-century Spanish nun like St. Teresa of Avila, can
only create disconnection, until at least some of them find a
way to talk about science and its seeming threat to religious
faith, or about what silence, prayer, and relationship (or
nonrelationship) to the church means in their own lives.

Reading Ourselves

Nothing is more crucial to teaching as spiritual practice
than replenishing the underground springs of a teacher's
own inner life. One teacher who has taught over thirty years
in elementary schools says this of the necessity of cultivating
her inner life, of reading herself:

> Teaching in elementary school is a very busy, demand-
> ing job, and I don't think I could have survived as a
> teacher were it not for my having developed an "inner
> life" to sustain and calm me in troubling situations. I
> didn't always remember to call on those inner
> resources, but my success in maintaining my own peace
> and stability was directly correlated to my remember-
> ing to pull back and draw on those inner resources.
> Every time I felt I had handled something badly, I
> thought "why didn't I take a minute to draw in a deep
> breath and pull back from the emotion of the moment
> before I responded?" Keeping that inner core of love,
> peace, calm, was just so important. And it wouldn't be
> there to call on if I failed to keep developing it through
> meditation.[31]

Transforming Relationship

If the banking method polarizes the relationship between teacher and student, resulting in too much authority on one side and too much submission on the other, in contemplative teaching the teacher gives up her authoritarian standpoint and risks openness to learning herself. Hierarchical, polarized methods of teaching keep teachers from experiencing students in depth and learning from them. Just as monarchical models of God encourage dependency, infantilism, and outright rebellion in their subjects, so it is with hierarchical models of teaching that echo these monarchical political and theological models.[32]

Teacher as *anam cara,* "soul friend" in the Celtic tradition, potentially breaks the impasse of too much or too little authority. The soul friend is a moral guide, one with inner authority, one who is willing to take the lead and risk the pilgrimage to the heart. The model of teacher as spiritual friend implies that the teacher calls upon his or her depth dimension, relationality, and openness to the sacred in the relationship with students; she is not merely "buddy" or worse. Authoritarianism and its mirror-opposite, blind obedience, are replaced by inner authority on both sides of the teacher-student polarity.

Transforming relationship entails making oneself vulnerable. As a young psychiatrist, Robert Coles learned that much of what he had put between himself and his patients were "protective theories." Just as I must learn who my students are, they learn who I am. An unspoken and often unacknowledged compact between student and teacher includes the student's expectation that the teacher is living the ideas and values she professes. Is she speaking off the top of her head or from her own deep rootedness in these values? Students have amazing radar for this congruency. How many of us acknowledge even to ourselves this unwritten and unspoken covenant and our failures to keep it? The teacher's—and learner's—integrity encompasses a wholeness of embodiment, thought, feeling, and vision, the same four elements that holistic education encourages in students.

Teaching as Unlearning: The Reading of God

Teaching is self-evidently a vocation of speaking, but it is not so often seen as a vocation of loosing and losing, using the chisels of questioning and even the soft chisel of silence to cut away old ideas and preconceptions. Where teaching encounters transcendence, it brings unlearning. Just as a monk had to pack up his belongings upon entering the monastery, the teaching vocation encompasses as much letting go as holding on, as much unlearning as learning. In order to reach the joy that Thomas Aquinas tells us accompanies contemplation, mystics and contemplatives say you proceed by the path of not-knowing. Perhaps the wisdom of the *via negativa* ("way of negation"), of unlearning, for a teacher can be summed up in one word: *kenosis,* or emptiness. We teachers continually confront what we do not know. In holding on to what we know, crystallizing and capsulizing it into theories and systems, we may have knowledge—which may even harden into dogma—but we lose the opportunity to search for wisdom. By not setting up and adoring idols of our own making, especially intellectual ones, we are in a way looking for, "reading," God and being "read" by God; we are being contemplatives.

But contemplation also involves a *kenosis* of those hard-won thoughts and categories so precious to us. Higher-order abstractions and conceptual frameworks organize reality for us! When I was working on a book on Gerard Manley Hopkins, for example, I not only learned about *kenosis;* I learned that I had to practice it in order to understand Hopkins fully. I learned from him to see and appreciate his realism, his being "in earnest with reality." When he spoke about Christ, Hopkins had another word for *kenosis;* he called it Christ's "chastity of mind." A chastity of the mind could mean keeping oneself clear and open, without prejudgments and opinions.

Impasse and Kenosis

Sometimes *kenosis* simply happens to us and doesn't have to be practiced. Life, too, with all its suffering and loss, becomes an excellent way of presenting lessons of this kind. Life teaches us through its impasse experiences, where we find no rational solution, and where immediate action only makes things worse: bad marriages, jobs that yield little fulfillment, peer pressures on the young, and, beyond these personal impasses, whole societal systems that have broken down. Wherever we look in the world today, at countries and institutions and relationships, we see this impasse. A contemporary Carmelite, Sr. Constance Fitzgerald, wrote a powerful essay twenty years ago that interprets our period of world history as a time of dark night, a time of impasse. Crises in corporate America, the Catholic Church, a war we did not foresee and that many of us did not want, are forcing us to seek deeper, less linear solutions.[33]

Whatever story I tell about my own spiritual journey has to make room for impasse and for suffering, the suffering of a whole people. That is because my father, grandfather, and unknown other members of my family suffered tremendously for no reason except that they were Jews. My father was picked up on *Kristallnacht*, the night of "broken glass," when synagogues and shops were destroyed and looted, and many Jews were rounded up for the camps. They were among the six million Jews who suffered in what is referred to now as the Holocaust. Such an enormous event of evil was and is an *impasse* for theology, destroying all our convenient pious images of God's love and mercy. Like Job in the Hebrew Bible, or like some theologians today, we can only shut our mouths in silence before the awful mystery of evil this event evokes. With no rational answer, no logical solution, it remains an impasse and a dark night from which we have not emerged. Divorce, loss of jobs and relationships, aspects of our identity we thought crucial, these are the desert places. They can bring a "dark night of the soul," a phrase which has entered into our common vocabulary from St. John of the Cross. John knew this experience really well, for when he was thrown into a dark prison cell by his own brother Carmelites, and stripped of everything external that could give life meaning, he found God, or rather God found him. In this utter wasteland of spirit and sense, he bloomed like a night flower, and wrote his *Spiritual Canticle*.

Confronted with students who do not seem to want to learn, who are nearly self-righteous about their ignorance, with principals and presidents who sometimes seem wedded to the status quo, many teachers today find themselves at an impasse. As students and teachers in our early years, we may have been too successful to learn from impasse, until one day we found ourselves with our heads buried in our hands, brooding over our students, our teaching, our lives. Sr. Constance Fitzgerald points out how inadequately our educational institutions equip us to deal with impasse: "As Americans we are not educated for impasse, for the experience of human limitation and darkness that will not yield to hard work, studies, statistics, rational analysis, and well-planned programs."[34] We all know these experiences, but we do not always know that we can be led through their darkness and emptiness. They force us out of analytical thinking and strip us of rational solutions, moving us into wholly new patterns of seeing and relating.

If teaching is to involve sustained joy, it must emerge on the other side of darkness and impasse, the very places where most of us now find ourselves. As anyone who has taken a spiritual route through a serious illness or loss knows, this very emptying-out, consciously and carefully undertaken, is preparation for ecstasy. William McNamara puts this well:

> The contemplative is easily pleased and deeply nourished precisely because he comes to the other empty-handed. It is hard for God or Beethoven to put anything into a closed fist. A cluttered mind or a crowded heart impedes the art of contemplation and therefore precludes any pleasurable consequences. That is why St. John of the Cross is so pitilessly hard on appetites. They fritter away our capacity for ecstasy.[35]

Because what I want for my students is this ecstasy, I invite them to sit in the paradox of knowing and unknowing, certainty and uncertainty, impasse and ecstasy.

Conclusion

The practices of contemplative teaching are in effect spiritual practices opening students and teachers who follow them to depth, relationality, and receptivity to the sacred. If we believe teaching can be a spiritual practice, that it contains within itself the seeds of contemplation, how do we re-imagine teaching along these lines? Guigo's ladder can help us name four practices in a transformed vocation of contemplative teaching for our time, and the remainder of this book will take up each of these in turn. Thus, from Guigo's reading we can be carried over to *attention*, from meditation to *reflection*, from prayer to *receptivity*, and from contemplation to *transforming vision*.

CHAPTER 2

Attention

May my teaching drop like the rain,
    my speech condense like the dew;
like gentle rain on grass,
    like showers on new growth.

—Deuteronomy 32:2

I would like now to bring Guigo and his ladder to the twenty-first century and introduce him into our classrooms in order to discover more precisely what contemplative teaching might look like. Guigo worked within an allegorical and metaphorical tradition of reading Scripture that actually valued correspondences between one world and another. In order to appreciate the richness of these stages as metaphor, we need to see them as Guigo's medieval contemporaries must have seen them: as fertile ground for the imagination. Metaphors "carried them across" (the literal meaning of *metaphor*) to a world of mystery and abundant meaning. So, in translating Guigo's metaphors for our time and teaching, we need not close down their meaning. The four practices that we are calling attention, reflection, receptivity, and transformation correspond, but only loosely, to the four rungs of the ladder Guigo wanted monks to climb.

Having said this, we still need to ground ourselves in the literal level of each of these practices, to lay a foundation for its metaphorical development. If we planted our feet firmly on the ladder's first rung of simple reading, we could hope to move up the ladder (or down as we might have it) to the others. Located as the first of the four rungs of Guigo's ladder, *lectio* entails the most basic and sensory of the acts that lead a monk to God. Without *lectio's* bottom rung of reading, there would be no opening to the mind's meditation, the heart's prayer, and the spirit's identity with the sacredness of it all. To avoid confusion, we will use *lectio* by itself for the first stage of reading and *lectio divina* for the fourfold process.

In this first step we actually engage the *body* in the work of contemplation. In the monastic period, *lectio* meant reading aloud, thereby almost tasting and savoring the words with one's mouth, a more physical act than our silent speed reading, and indeed a kind of body prayer.[1] It was gustatory and earthy, "like a grape that is put into the mouth filled with many senses to feed the soul."[2] For Hugh of St. Victor, another twelfth-century monk, the page (*pagina,* meaning "vineyard") was a place to pick and taste its "berries," the words. *Lectio* feels like the child's putting out its hands to touch and taste the world, giggling with delight that the world is there at all and full of delicious tastes. A striking feature of this pre-Cartesian era was the intimate relation between the body's sensory experience and the soul. If *lectio* was a more physical act than our silent reading, it was also more spiritual in the sense that the body was the means of the soul's awakening. *Lectio* then involves a basic act of attention or "presentness," a coming to our senses. Attention can be purposefully intransitive (attention to what?) and therefore open-ended.

With reality becoming more virtual all the time, with texts evaporating into cyberspace, the very materiality and focus of the book is a comfort. In Guigo's twelfth century, biblical texts, handwritten on translucent parchment and richly illuminated, were more palpable objects, objects with "texture." When appropriated in the spirit of *lectio divina*, the texts of Scripture pointed beyond themselves to the holy. What began in an earthy way, holding and ruminating with this physical book, led all the way to heaven. It takes humility (from *humus,* earth) to tune in to God in ordinary time and space. The simple act of reading in such a context and with such intent led a person to transformative encounter with God. What Ivan Illich says of Hugh we might also say of Guigo and the whole tradition of *lectio divina*:

> He still walks through the pages and conceives of reading as a pilgrimage. Reading is not solely a visual activity for him, not an accumulation. Rather, reading is a pilgrimage towards regions ever lighter, towards the light, into the light, until the light becomes so strong that he doesn't go on reading but begins to contemplate.[3]

Wandering through the vineyard, stopping to taste its rich fruit, constituted not only the experience of reading but a wayside shrine on the journey towards God. Now how can we teachers and learners make our literal and metaphorical reading into a pilgrimage toward the light again?

Benedict's *Lectio* in Teaching: Attention

We have said that the spiritual practice of attention brings us into the present moment. In the teacher's presence to the moment and in the student's attention, all three aspects of spiritual practice—the psychological depth of returning to ourselves, relating to others, and not-doing—are found. In teaching, we usually formulate the problem of attention in terms of getting students to "pay" attention. All the way up the line from elementary to post-secondary school, we tell our students, as we were told, to pay attention. Perhaps the metaphor reveals a kind of exchange: you pay (attention) and I will pay (in grades); or, if you don't pay (attention), you will pay (the price). The commodification of knowledge becomes the commodification of attention. Is it any wonder that diagnoses of "attention deficit disorders" and now "attention deficit hyperactive disorders" abound, when we live in a hyperactive society overstimulated with attention-grabbers? I have watched children go from videos to computer games to television shows and back, their attention colonized, their minds never having a chance to rest and replenish through play. Lack of depth seems the inevitable consequence of this continual flashing of flat images before them. We can give students no greater gift than the present moment, for only in the present can we know Thomas Aquinas' joy and wonder of contemplation and the depth of Benedict's and Guigo's *lectio*. To one awakening to the energy and vitality of life, the world "is charged with the grandeur of God. / It will flame out like shining from shook foil."[4]

But the present moment is the last place we in the West seem to be as we enter the new millennium. In our increasingly frantic world, where we move at more and more dizzying speeds just to get by, we rarely stop to give our attention. In the active life of teaching, an inevitable occupational hazard is busyness, if not sheer franticness. As the poet David Whyte puts it, "The hurried child becomes the pressured student, and finally the harassed manager [read teacher!]....The process is begun very young and can be so in our bones...that the inability to pay real attention to our world may be difficult to recognize."[5]

In addition to time and its pace is distance, "estrange-ment." We are walled off from nature and other people; even though "the world is charged with the grandeur of God,...the soil / Is bare now, nor can foot fell, being shod" (from Gerard Manley Hopkins' "God's Grandeur"). How many of us can say of whatever or whoever we attend to what Guigo said about the function of reading: "There may be something good here. I shall return to my heart and try to understand and find this purity, for this is indeed a precious and desirable thing."[6]

Although we often complain about lack of attention in our students, we teachers, along with our students, need to wake up to what is really there. Without the practice of pres-ence, we may never know who is really before us on any given day, or indeed, know who it is who teaches. Is it the wife still inwardly arguing with her husband? The father worried about his own child's illness or separation anxiety? The teacher nursing a grudge against the administration, or furious with the students' lack of motivation? Preoccupied either with past hurts or future plans, or wrapped in com-forting illusions but unable to acknowledge them, I am sometimes just not there. Presence is, in Sharon Solloway's words, not "a calculated attempt to practice concern for oth-ers or concern for self, rather, presence...points to the wis-dom of *wu-wei*—the attempt to move with events as they arise, keenly observing and letting action then be the com-plement to what is observed."[7] The first step on the ladder of *lectio divina* returns the mind to the body from the outer space of our mental excursions. We can check in with our bodies to sense the tensions, the unease in the stomach, stiff necks from overwork, or tightness as if bracing for a fight.

So how do we teachers become truly attentive when so much mental and emotional baggage drags us away? Perhaps we can learn from one group of teachers, from kindergarten through high school, who experimented with contemplative practice both in and out of the classroom.[8] First, they practiced sitting meditation at home thirty minutes a day for eight weeks. As a consequence of this meditation, they brought a different quality of attention, a mindfulness, into their classrooms. Mindfulness—attention—opened a space between themselves and their experience in the classroom, "a pre-signifying space in which what is happening is experienced without words attached."[9] Surprisingly, their attentiveness made them less prepared to assign labels to situations and students, less "armed" in fact. They came disarmed. Where I might want to prepare myself with mental notes like "difficult class" (or "class from hell"), they have shed such armor, only to be more open, less defended, less tight. This kind of attention involves suspending judgment and tolerating ambiguity, opening awareness to more of what is happening. These "contemplative practitioners" found what Thomas Merton has called the "space of liberty...in which possibilities are allowed to surface and new choices—beyond routine choice—become manifest."[10] Perhaps when Jesus said, "Do not judge, so that you may not be judged" (Matt 7:1), he meant practice attention—be present and awake.

Those teachers practicing contemplative awareness through meditation recorded their experiences of attention in journal entries.[11] One who had seen himself before as "student-centered" said,

> I'm learning to back away from my wired style and let other things happen. This takes a lot less energy....You know it's comfortable to be dictatorial. But it's not as effective. I'm learning to be more flexible, but I'm thinking, "Oh, if I do this, I'm going to lose control." Control, that's the big issue.

Another, who had just been told about an attack on a teacher friend, entered her own classroom and watched her body become rigid with rage as she saw the children gathered in a circle around her. She describes what happened as she drew in her breath and then let it out,

> I let all of that drain out, and just kind of went back to that quiet place. In just a few seconds, happy and comfortable, everything fit. I could go back to what I knew was my plan, and what I knew the children needed to get out of this phonics lesson.[12]

Instead of giving in to rage, a natural reaction to the story of the attack, this teacher entered a space of greater freedom and possibility, including what "fit" this moment of being present to her students. She was not trapped in reactivity. Rather than repress or express her anger, she gave it nonjudgmental attention, letting it pass through her body and dissolve.[13] In another example, a teacher who changed from elementary to middle school thought she had to don a sterner personality to keep the students in line. As she brought nonjudgmental attention to her internal and external experiences in the classroom, she found herself lightening up:

> I was so tight, exhausted, but this was like letting go, just letting go. My body felt so light. And I was so aware of everything I was doing, my facial movements as I spoke, arm movements, and my legs as I walked around the room. And everything [the students] were doing, but all of it was easy, not hard and tight. It's noticing more detail—student to student and teacher to student. I have more insight and connection with my students. I pick up on subtle things I didn't before. I note expressions of confusion more often. I was seeing each of my kids...rather than this is my fourth hour class, here THEY are.[14]

"More...connection with my students," is a wonderful testimony to the empathy of attention. In these examples, the teacher's *lectio* is more like a diffused awareness of the whole than a laser-pointed focus on one thing, such as one student's bad behavior or the teacher's own reactive anger. She reads the moment's internal and external, subjective and objective qualities, not settling for a "take" on reality that only takes away its fullness. These teachers realize that thoughts, especially judgments, keep us from being present. As one educational theorist put it, "More of the complexity that is the nature of all things tempers our rush to define with a brutal, fixed identity the Other we encounter."[15]

Among feminist philosophers, the notion of attention has opened up an important conversation in recent years. Simone Weil first connected attention with both prayer and "school studies."[16] For Annie Dillard, its total concentration is "pure devotion to an object." For Martha Nussbaum it means being "finely aware and richly responsible." Pure devotion, rich responsibility, these are simply other ways of speaking of love. For Josephine Donovan the epistemology of attention entails an ethic that is "non-imperialistic, life-affirming, and that reverences the concrete details of life." And Daniel Hardy speaks of the *dignity* attention confers on the one who attends.[17] Attention reminds us that the simple act of *lectio,* being present enough to see or listen, may be the hardest act of all.

Returning to Ourselves

Our greatest spiritual problem today may be the addictions to work and tasks that keep us from looking at ourselves. Professorial absent-mindedness is nearly a trademark of the profession, almost a certifying characteristic. A story is told of an Oxford don meeting another on a walk and the first asking the second if he had had lunch. The second don replied by asking which way he was going when they met.

When the first pointed out the way, the other don replied, "Well, then, I had lunch." If this story illustrates what some might find an admirable detachment from things of sense, it also demonstrates how far this teacher has come from his own body and from the present moment. For many of us it is a great temptation to escape into words, and more recently into cyberspace, never returning to ourselves. I periodically need to stop and ask myself, what am I using—the computer, the TV, doing class preparation—to keep me from myself, my soul? In contrast, the monks of the Middle Ages placed the phrase *Age quod agis* ("do what you are doing") over their doors as a reminder to be fully present to the act of eating, sleeping, and praying. This dictum probably applied to reading too. The monastic imperative of *age quod agis* echoes the Zen saying: "When I am eating, I am eating." So the first act of attention necessitates returning to ourselves, our bodies, and our own depths. In each of the examples of contemplative practitioners cited above, the teacher became more aware of himself or herself. If we have scattered our attention and cannot be with ourselves in this fundamental way, we cannot be with others. The so-called Prodigal Son serves as an archetype of the person who catches himself up in a relentless pursuit of distractions and then returns to himself (Luke 15:17). Only then can he turn to the father who loves him.

Emptying

When attention has become such a scarce commodity, we cannot simply ask students to pay attention.[18] Not the "payment" of attention, but the practice of a *poverty of spirit* is in order when there is nothing left to pay. The sort of muscular effort and moral imperative implied in paying attention will not work unless we have asked ourselves and our students to do the inner works of spiritual practice: returning to the *depths* of the heart, emptying by *not-doing,* and *relating* to what is really there. While most middle-class Americans are becoming more plugged-in all the time, the deliberate emptiness of unplugging seems an odd antidote. A news magazine reported that 39 percent of those who watch TV regularly complain of depression, while about the same percentage who use that time to engage in hobbies do not. Boredom is the failure of attention. Yet "boring" is unfortunately the verdict so many of our students give when we ask them to give even more attention. I once asked a class of seniors in discussing Simone Weil's assertion that "the joy of learning is as indispensable in study as breathing," why they did not experience this joy. They answered unanimously that it was because their *teachers* and classes were boring. Their real need was not for more stimulation, but less, for an emptying out of their overfilled attentions.

Deliberate emptying differs greatly from the emptiness and boredom that result from over- and under-stimulation. What we have been calling *kenosis,* based on Jesus' emptying of Godhead in accepting his humanity (Phil 2:6–11), belongs to attention. *Kenosis* (emptying) appears a harsh, almost purgative, remedy for the collusion between our entertainment culture and its all-too-willing participants. The conclusion seems inescapable: We can give our attention only when it is not enslaved by everything else. The cleansing of attention by creating a "space of liberty," one not in thrall to the latest consumer fad, could cure this ennui. Attention frees us from the enslavement to idols.

In a world continuously letting us down, the theological virtue of faith is essential to attention. We need faith that the world is indeed worthy of our "yes." We are used to negotiating our worlds through heavy doses of irony, a self-protective "no" preventing us from being taken in by the world's betrayals. Irony, an attitude that has survived both modern and postmodern criticism, prevents assent to the real. Attention is particularly difficult for intellectuals who hold the world at bay with their irony. Today, bred on irony and fed a constant supply of shocks, we are losing our ability to be surprised, to be delighted. Attention operates, as it were, in neutral, giving up both the fantasies and expectations that prescribe what we *want* to be there and the irony that rejects what *is* there. Without attention, we and our students miss the moment of wonder, miss the chance to *meet* and *attend* our subjects, dismiss the training in reverence that it could bring.

The contemplative gesture of attention goes beyond an acknowledgment of being to an act of affirmation and assent that says "yes" with a delight that leads to joy. Attention involves an uncluttered *appreciation* of the existence of a thing. Jesus' *emptying* and his *acceptance* are, in fact, the twin dynamics of the practice of attention. The contemplative gesture of appreciation can help counter the pervasive feeling that what we have is not enough.

Attention, with its assent, brings reverence for being and life, even and especially if it is useless. The fourteenth-century visionary woman, Julian of Norwich, provides a classic example of attention in her famous episode with the hazelnut. Walled within her anchorage, Julian turns her attention to something with no apparent significance. And yet in the hazelnut she encounters "everything that is made," the very mystery of Being itself. Is it any wonder that Julian saw God and Jesus as mother, for the mother's attention often goes to what is seemingly useless and insignificant. Julian's experience involves the great paradox of attention: the clearer and emptier one's attention is, the more it allows in. It is like the eye of the needle that lets one into heaven.

We can convey the gift of attention to students if we make a place for it first in ourselves, and then in the curriculum. We cannot give our acceptance to this moment, we cannot open ourselves, until we empty ourselves of the crowd of intruders barring the door to it. In her essay on "school studies," the philosopher-mystic Simone Weil describes well the *kenosis* necessary for attention: "The soul empties itself of all its own contents in order to receive into itself the being it is looking at, just as [it] is, in all [its] truth." *Attention* to our school studies effects a self-diminishing awakening to what *is* rather than what we want to be. The thinking inherent in attention should be "empty, waiting, not seeking anything." Not only that, but our quality of attention can make even the mundane act of study prayerful, according to Weil. Thought of in this way, says Weil, our studies become "like a sacrament."[19]

Apprenticing oneself to a tradition and to the rigorous discipline of a method—in science, math, social science, or humanities—becomes one way of learning the detachment and *kenosis* necessary for attention. When we seize upon an answer prematurely we make mistakes, blocking the truth from coming in its own time. As hard as it is, *waiting* (for the right word or answer to come, or for the soul in front of us to emerge in its own time), not frantic seeking, is the heart of attention. The Taoist term *wu wei* ("doing without doing") is appropriate here, for *wu wei* steps back from dominating the experience in word or act and lets the actor move spontaneously into events as they happen. This waiting on the other relates us more authentically to the other. Attention is quite naturally "compassionate time" that makes time for another.

Relatedness

Some philosophers, like those cited earlier, have seen attention as the first act of love, and this understanding emphasizes the element of acceptance in attention.

Commenting on attention in her philosophical writing, the late Oxford don Iris Murdoch says: "The direction of attention…[must be] away from self which reduces all to a false unity, toward the great surprising variety of the world, and the ability to so direct attention is love."[20] Iris Murdoch's novels are full of characters who construct their lives on fantasies and projections and then experience *moments of attention* when the blinders of projections fall away, and they see the other person as if for the first time. Only then can the possibility of love exist. In Simone Weil's essay on attention, she suggests that doing a geometry problem or working on Latin prose with "attention"—even if we are not very good at them—can someday enable one to respond to a neighbor in affliction: "Those who are unhappy have no need for anything in this world but people capable of giving them their attention."[21] Our attentiveness to the world's surprising multiplicity deconstructs our own false unity, even if our identity is the "nice person" or "good teacher." What is critical, situated at the *crisis* between self-confirmation and otherness, is empathy with the other.[22]

Perhaps it is not too great a leap to go from Simone Weil's attention to school studies to attention in the classroom. Whether looking with a microscope at a single-celled amoeba, scanning a poem, or solving a complex mathematical formula, students find the classroom a place for attending. And we need to bring in all meanings of the word. Attending can mean "waiting upon," as those gathered around a chemical experiment in the lab know well; it can also mean caring for, as an attendant cares for someone, and those in the nursing profession know this image well. As contemplative teachers and learners, we become *attendants* to the realities we invite into our contemplative space. As a contemplative teacher, I can know whether my students are with me or not, or whether I may need to give up my carefully prepared lecture and lesson plans to be with them where they are. Sometimes they give me huge hints with body language (the "hat guys" in the back) or with questions, but sometimes not. I struggle to see and appreciate where my students are. In graduate school, when I wanted to promulgate my own ideas, my professors continually reminded me to give a faithful account of what each author was saying, to give these authors attention. I am grateful to them now. But in this age of strong interpreters and their successors, the deconstructionists, such faithfulness is in short supply.

A necessary condition for becoming contemplative in our teaching involves the ability to see what is worthy of our attention and to deny the rest entrance. On the other hand, if we wish our attention to be *just,* as well as loving, we need to give more attention to those previously overlooked in the composition of our curricula. We need to be aware of the *null curriculum,* comprising the peoples and subjects and processes (such as rituals) that are left out of a too Western, too cerebral course of study. Contemplative teaching acknowledges the tension between teaching from the established canon and including those who have been left out: women, ordinary people, people of color, all who experience themselves as living on the margins or the underside of history. At the same time, it affirms that teaching, if it is responsible and alive, takes place within these tensions, but still maintains a calmer search for wisdom and meaning.

Contemplative teaching schools us in a different relationship to the objects of one's concern: not subject-object domination, but subject-subject dialogue, where the subject is a true *subject,* with a voice of its own that can also teach us. It is not an *object,* not something thrown out and over against us, as Parker Palmer reminds us; it stands alongside us as equal, as teacher. Attention is the practice, then, of faithfulness and doing justice—to the author, the text, the reality before us.

Some Concrete Proposals
in Restoring Attention

- Clear a space around students and within students, both physically and mentally.
- Create downtime—unstructured, unplanned, open to discovery.
- Unplug laptops, VCRs, and TVs in the classroom.
- Spend time in nature and let the natural world speak to you.

CHAPTER 3

Reflection

And all of us, with unveiled faces, seeing the glory of the
Lord as though reflected in a mirror, are being transformed into the same image from one degree of glory to
another.

—2 Corinthians 3:18

In the schema Guigo proposes for monks—the ladder he
hopes they will ascend—meditation occupies the second
rung. Meditation for Guigo "is the busy application of the
mind to seek with the help of one's own reason for knowledge of hidden truth."[1] Each word in this definition, unlike
the other stages of the whole process of *lectio divina*, could
work in an educational context. This stage *by itself* fits well
into academic settings that separate head and heart, reason
and feeling, sacred and secular. Reason is the very lifeblood
of the academy and of the school, but its lifeblood is a thin
one, one that circulates mostly in the head. Unlike monastic
settings, where meditation was rooted in scriptural reading,
the scholasticism of medieval universities increasingly tended
to lift this rung right off the ladder and make it stand alone
as a platform unto itself, where it is today. I think here espe-

cially of the medieval philosopher Abelard's *Sic et Non* ("Yes and No") that juxtaposed contradictory statements from the church fathers and from Scripture in a pure reasoning process. In a sense, then, it did not go anywhere, certainly not on to the "journey of the heart," the destiny of *lectio divina*.

We in the postmodern age experience the impoverishment of the Enlightenment ideal of reason *alone*, and are abandoning those ideals as a culture and as individuals. Reason has served us so well as a laser tool in overcoming prejudice, ignorance, and error, that we would be foolish to abandon it. Yet, a "shrunken rationality," to use philosopher Elizabeth Minnich's phrase, a rationality lacking emotion, embodiment, spirit, and intuition, deadens our spirits.[2] The very inadequacy of reason when it is up against the great mysteries of life could lead us to a humility that could open the heart. Often we see this humility among the great physicists of our time, and among doctors who must accept death as a natural chapter of life. And yet, in near defiance and denial, the academy remains a bastion of reason alone. The question remains, how can we make our learning heart-filled, and how can we say with the medieval monastic writers, *Amor ipse est notitia* ("Love itself is knowledge")?[3] How do we bring back the heart to our educational enterprises?

Guigo, our monastic guide to contemplation, intended an integral movement between the steps of *lectio divina*.

> Reading, as it were, puts food whole into the mouth, meditation chews it and breaks it up, prayer extracts its flavor, contemplation is the sweetness itself which gladdens and refreshes. Reading works on the outside, meditation on the pith: prayer asks for what we long for, contemplation gives us delight in the sweetness which we have found.[4]

Far from an intellectual exercise, meditation is related to the whole of the life of prayer in an organic way. So meditation chews, even masticates, on the fare that has been offered in *lectio*. Monastic writers were fond of the metaphor of rumination for this stage in the process, calling up an image of the cow slowly ruminating its cud out in the field. Even today the dictionary tells us that to ruminate is "to think deeply about something." The great ideas are *ruminated,* both fed to us and brought up for continuous reflection. Guigo shows us the necessity of this second act in implanting the text within the heart: "For what is the use of spending one's time in continuous reading [of books]...unless we can extract nourishment from them by chewing and digesting this food so that its strength can pass into our inmost heart?"[5] What a question this remains for us in the twenty-first century who often waste time consuming documents both material and virtual, not allowing them to nourish us deeply. The trouble is, we are both overfed and undernourished. We gulp down ideas without reflection just as we gulp down fast food.

If for monks *lectio* means tasting the grapes of the vineyard of Scripture, meditation is "as though putting [them] in a wine press," extracting their precious juices and savoring their flavors until they diffuse our being deeply.[6] These monks probably made their own wine, and knew full well the delightful odor of grapes pressed into intoxicating juices! For them, meditation takes the grapes of experience and puts them into the winepress of reflection, releasing their full potency. Without the movement into reflection, we never reach the depths of ourselves, the still center, in effect the truth. If we are to cultivate thoughtfulness, we need the contemplative winepress of meditation, reasoning, and reflection to assimilate the contents of our experiences. And for Guigo, just as meditation works to press out ideas so that we can assimilate them, it functions to kindle and fan the intellectual sparks into flames of a transforming fire, a passion.[7] Seeing what is there in attention, imbibing it, and then kindling its sparks into "a fire in the belly" in reflection constitute the first stages of a contemplative teaching modality.

Meditation East and West

When we hear the word *meditation* today, we think of the Eastern forms of meditation so prevalent in this country. Eastern meditation empties the mind of thoughts and images and feelings. By contrast, in the West *meditation* has often meant actively applying the intellect, will, and affections to the meditative subject. What the West understands as *contemplation,* where the mind leaves behind active thinking and loses itself in God, is closer to Eastern meditation. Both the active and quiet mental processes are found in the word *meditation (hagah),* which originated within the Jewish context, where Scripture was recited in Temple and synagogue:

> The monastic practice of *lectio* inherits the Jewish way of reading Scripture that formed part of an indivisible unity of prayer. The root Hebrew word *hagah* is translated as "meditation" in most translations of the Bible and, as the Midrash states, it is the "heart," not the mind, that meditates. *Hagah* denotes both interiorization (["Let the words of my mouth and the meditation of my heart be acceptable to you, O Lord"] Ps 19:14) and repetition or "murmuring" of the sacred words (Ps 35:20; Isa 38:14). This suggests a practice of prayer entirely comparable to the repetition of a mantra in Asian traditions.[8]

The Jewish tradition's *hagah*—meditation—of certain sacred words approaches the use of the mantra in Eastern methods of meditation to focus and steady the mind. Even more, the Jewish and then the monastic traditions see meditation as engaging the *heart*. When monks spoke of the meditative stage of *lectio divina,* one biblical parallel prevailed: Mary "treasured and pondered" in her heart the words of the angels and shepherds (Luke 2:19). The heart's meditation digs deeper than a merely mental one. To meditate, then, is to let the words tap gently and repeatedly on the door of the heart, to lay that which has claimed our attention on the heart, the center of the whole personality. In Jewish *hagah,* to say, "I will meditate on your words in my heart," as the psalmist does, is to say, "I will repeat these words until they break in upon my heart and change it." Our very repetition, though frustrating to the aggressive, linear mind, purges the mind of its impatient need to get somewhere. That is the way poetry works, and why poems can slow us down enough to be present and awake. Just reciting the psalms can have this effect for me, as one or two words manage to grab hold of my runaway attention.

In his study of the Western tradition of prayer, Michael Casey, a Cistercian monk of Australia, captures this sense of *meditatio*:

> In the Middle Ages, the *meditatio* was not restricted to mental activity....More like a friendship, a cherishing, whereby one lived with a text that had become particularly dear, exploring it from different vantage points, saying it to oneself in a quiet, non-analytic way and letting it act on the heart.[9]

In our academic settings today, it is difficult to remember that the critical intellect was once connected to the whole self, especially the heart. Reflection in educational contexts too often becomes the temptation to overidentify with and get stuck in thought without hope of going beyond it: "They perished in their own ideas," as Guigo succinctly puts it, echoing Paul.[10] After the sixteenth century and the Enlightenment, the mind's intimate kinship with the heart and the body came apart, and so too did the nonanalytic "friend-ship" and "cherishing" of texts and topics to which this stage was meant to bring us. Amazingly, the new study of neuroscience seems to be reknitting this body-mind connection by exploring the way emotions, as physiological events, give rise to feelings and to thoughts.[11] Through a contemplative reflection, it is still possible to engage the intellect in concert with the whole person who is thinking.

Guigo's Meditation in Teaching: Reflection

Adopting Guigo's metaphor for our academic setting, as we "chew" the grapes of experience of the empirical world, we blend them into ourselves as well, becoming one with what we know. As we catch and kindle the sparks of ideas from the vast stores of knowledge that have preceded us in the tradition, or from the contemporary world, our reflection brings those dead embers alive in us. To quote Hopkins once more, "blue-bleak embers, ah my dear, / Fall, gall themselves and gash gold-vermilion" (from "The Windhover"). Reflection, the act of inward understanding, without which we make no real connection with ourselves, begins to embed the subject in the very person of the hearer or reader.

Reflection and the Image of God

Reflection is a great privilege, manifesting the dignity of the image of God that is our human birthright. The God-given ability to reflect gives voice to a sacred individuality, one not co-opted by the dominant ideology, one not able to be colonized, even by educators. That is why it will always seem dangerous. Immersion in the collective makes us unwilling to take personal responsibility for what we think and feel and do, and so unwilling to reflect deeply.[12]

Reflection gives the lie to the absolutizing of a *social* construction of knowledge, for it gives rise to the new, the creative, the original. Originally, the little root *flex* in the word *reflection* meant "bending back or again." As we flex the muscles of intellect and reason, the active side of *reflex*-ion, we begin to break away from conventional fixations. Yet, this reflection muscle must itself be flexed, so as not to become dogmatically stuck. Guigo himself expected that in meditation "we would carefully consider our state of soul."[13] For all of us, reflection involves the turn from being *right* to seeking truth, even to what Gandhi called "experiments with Truth." Reflection, especially when it involves self-reflection, is the practice of freedom, of challenging even our most basic assumptions, our worldviews.

Not all teachers can bring meditation into their classrooms daily, but some form of reflection seems a necessity for vital nurture by subjects and ideas. Reflection, indeed all learning, is an instinct as natural as chewing. Yet, although it is a privilege of us primates, we still manage to resist it mightily because it opens the way to *change*, a scary prospect. Fear, the fear of whatever attitudes, assumptions, or prejudices might need to change, precludes reflection. Students' resistance to thinking is legendary. Who has not heard the student's implicit or explicit cry, "You're making me think!" School, especially in the later years, is a great place to learn *not* to think or reflect, but to take refuge instead in the thought of credentialed authorities or teachers. School is a hideout for thinking in such an objective, other-centered way that it never involves us in self-reflection.

Paradoxically, though, reflection that is part of an integral process means *connection* as well as freedom, believing as well as doubting, like breathing in and breathing out. Seeing reflection in the context of *lectio divina,* related to what comes before and what comes after, makes it more holistic, a practice that ends not in separation but in love. With reflection, the hardening of the intellectual arteries gives way to a softening of the heart. If the Enlightenment taught us to be detached, objective knowers, stepping away from the object of our study, this kind of knowing reverses the direction by moving us toward and even into it. In a way, all knowing involves separation, the separateness of knower and known, begun in the Garden of Eden with Adam's objective and alienated knowing of himself, his wife, and God. But contemplative knowing moves us toward healing the separation. In contemplation, we reflect to connect. As one interpreter of contemplation explains it: "Reasoning tends to separate, for it involves a subject thinking and an object thought about....Awareness, which is central to contemplation, is a very different experience from thinking: it tends always to be unitive...The contemplative sees everything in unity and therefore rejects any dualism that would separate God from creation."[14] Contemplative reflection increases awareness of ourselves and our world.

Reflection and Time

But reflection takes time. We need "the illusion of infinite time," as the late Paul Connolly, of Bard College's Institute of Language and Thinking, used to say. The linear paradigm that has us all in its grip—especially in the classroom— makes us feel that we must continually move on, and follow a hidden but compelling straight line to some distant goal. In so doing, we nearly always neglect the *re* in reflection. The *re* ("back" or "again") in reflection means we must circle back, return to ourselves and our subjects, going deeper each time. One wonders what sort of educational rollercoaster we are providing students that prevents their taking a minute for self-reflection. We must try at least to pretend that time is not a straight line, but a continuously widening and deepening spiral. Although reflection takes time, it gives it back, reducing the needless spinning of wheels. Time for reflection is *kairos,* not clock time but that time-out-of-time that loses track of time. Because it is a natural function, reflection happens of itself when conditions allow it to happen, when we stop filling the time. Allowing reflection to happen in our classrooms, and encouraging it outside of them, whether in the leaves of books or the leaves of nature, would be a powerful teaching that clock time is not all there is, that the eternal can break through.

Our children are the real experts at reflection, at the daydreams and reveries that enable them to "think outside the box" or color outside the lines, often to their teachers' consternation. So, how can we become "as a little child" again (Luke 18:17), and how can our *disciplines* reflect and not squelch this wonderful talent? How can we create a disciplined daydreaming? When one group of teachers met at the "Education and the Spirit" conference in 1996, in a session called "Making Friends with Silence,"[15] among the many suggestions for creating silent reflection in the classroom were these: writing pauses; cards for questions at the end of class; "ah-ha papers"—describing how the body, feelings, and intellect feel at the moment of insight; *rituals* involving breathing; music; dimmed lights; opening and closing circles; chanting; bodily gestures to express the inner movement of thought; dancing; eating; contemplation of an object; saying a line of poetry while walking; drawing, sculpting, and writing an insight; freewriting, where seemingly meaningless thoughts can coalesce into real insights; compiling a spiritual autobiography in some form, even collages of your life depicted on a mandala. An award-winning mathematics teacher at a Texas high school, Cindy Boyd, puts the process of reflection this way:

> Most of the time we go through a discovery process. I
> play the devil's advocate so they're kind of teaching me,

explaining the concept to me. First we summarize our findings in our own words, we talk about the idea, about what we discovered, until it's pretty well crystallized. Then we go through it in a skit where it is further crystallized, and then in a song, where we play with it and have fun with it. And then we may follow that with a card game or a worksheet to give them some practice.[16]

Recalling the characteristics of a contemplative teaching style as psychological and spiritual *depth, relatedness* to the other, and receptivity to *transcendence,* I would like to propose the kind of reflection that (1) draws from the depths of its own well, (2) is capable of connecting and mirroring its subject (and students) faithfully, and (3) contemplates the transcendent mystery of life and being itself. With its depth dimension, reflectiveness opens a person to herself or himself; with its relatedness, it opens to another; and with its potential for transcendence, it can open one to God.

Digging the Well: Depth

In our classrooms, some form of ritual can bridge the gap between an unreflective formation, merely indoctrinating young people into established norms, and reflection on new pathways, moving into a new relation to their lives. Rituals that integrate body with spirit and individuals into a community create a space for reflection. We can make space in our classes, crowded as they are, for a ritual coming together to become a class and to decide who we will be and how each of us will be responsible to others. The ritual of consensus-building, passing a "talking-stick" or talisman, can invite already reflective individuals into sharing their thoughts with and creating community. And ritual need not be ritualistic, in a formal and rigid sense. The English theologian and housewife, Rosemary Haughton, defines ritual simply as people doing something together on purpose and *meaning* something by it—creating the opportunity for transformation. An ordinary family meeting in their living room to make a decision about their future is engaging in ritual action: having been called together for a purpose, "their action was in itself an expression of membership in the family, and of a sense of responsibility towards it....This is ritual."[17] We can do this in our classrooms. We can imagine "rituals of reflection" occurring in the conventional space of the classroom, but transforming it.

The notion of reflection conjures up for me images of deep wells and clear lakes. With these metaphors, we can understand reflection as thought irrigated from within. St. Teresa of Avila has a beautiful image of two water troughs:

> These two troughs are filled with water in different ways; with one the water comes from far away through many aqueducts and the use of much ingenuity; with the other the source of the water is right there, and the trough fills without any noise. If the spring is abundant...the water overflows once the trough is filled, forming a large stream. There is no need of any skill, nor does the building of aqueducts have to continue, but water is always flowing from the spring.[18]

Although Teresa meant these images to refer to states of meditation in prayer, we can see how readily they apply to the art of teaching. The first trough, with its intermittent and dependent aqueduct systems necessary to bring in water, depicts the student's dependence on exterior sources of knowledge, on the teacher in fact, while the second resembles the ability to draw from one's own well of insight and reflection. In fact, our monastic writer Guigo also uses the metaphor of the well for meditation: "I feel that 'the well is deep,' but I am still an ignorant beginner, and it is only with difficulty that I have found something in which to draw up these few drops."[19] If our solitary monk has difficulty begin-

ning to reflect, how much more so our utterly besieged students and educators! Our wells run dry so often without the inner springs of reflection.

In this era of test obsession, if we teachers believe going to the well of deep reflection is a luxury we and our students cannot afford, we can look to the greatest scientists of our time, such as Albert Einstein. In our day, the best models of reflection may be scientists who sit with and ponder an experiment or problem, seeing deeper into it little by little. Einstein's theory of relativity actually began with the inner play of images and free invention of ideas. When asked what constitutes the mind of a mathematician, Einstein described images and signs that appeared "voluntarily," and that he could "play with." His well of reflection was filled with images, not primarily with a program or method. Einstein often spoke to the need for intuition and imagination, not systematic logic, as the basis for theoretical physics, saying,

> The state of mind which enables a [person] to do work of this kind is akin to that of the religious worshiper or the lover; the daily effort comes from no deliberate intention or program, but straight from the heart.[20]

Some of the greatest scientific theories of our age were discovered by going to the well, even to the well of dreams. One German scientist, Frederick Kekule (1829–1896) had a dream of a serpent biting its tail, and when he awakened, he had discovered the chemical structure of benzine which had eluded him until then.[21] I believe these scientists' ability to trust their own insights arose from their willingness to go to their own well of reflection, even in the face of much contrary conventional wisdom.

A contemporary teacher in the sciences explains the value of having students reflect on ways to explain a certain technique to peers in small groups (4–6 people) or discussions sections (15–25 people): "The amount of energy put into preparation for those presentations and the understanding taking place surpasses all the things I could do for the students by lecturing to them....The students generate their own questions, research them and return to what they've found with their peers."[22]

What happens for our students when they are given the opportunity to reflect? For students, going to the well means deep learning. Deep learning involves proceeding from surface acquisition of facts and memorization of formulas to an appropriation at deeper and deeper levels of one's self. It opens a path to meaning. *Meaning* literally kept Victor Frankl alive during the nightmare of the concentration camps. Although classrooms should surely *not* be compared with concentration camps, even for students, when students get a draught of meaning, you can see how utterly life-giving it is, like opening a wellspring within.

Emptying the Well

In order to dig the well of self, it must first be cleared. Some of the reflection we encourage in students, then, ought to clear a space and cleanse the heart of distortions and delusions. One great tool for emptying out those dogmas, prejudices, and media images that cloud students' minds and prevent learning is the *question*, but just for that reason it can involve a shattering of idols that is painful. For students, doubting and critical thinking aid purification by clearing away mental and dogmatic images. Questions can act like pinpricks in the conceptual bubbles that even we teachers surround ourselves with to feel safe, for, as Lao Tzu once said, "he who feels deflated must once have been a bubble." Though a question may bring down an entire value system and leave it hanging deflated around us, it can allow us to step out of this old system and into something more real. When teachers ask questions of their subjects, they stand again at the boundaries of knowledge, leaning into new territory. At the same time, they mirror the questioning of their subjects for students. Questions clear away incrustations of untruth so that something of truth can stand forth. Much of reflection might mean listening for the questions that everyone has been too afraid, or too confident, to ask. I learned quickly in memorizing the *Baltimore Catechism* during my grade school years that questions were frowned upon, perhaps because they were seen as opening the door to a doubt considered incompatible with faith.

Questions remain critical—yet if all we do is try to develop our students' critical thinking skills, we leave them in an indeterminate no-man's-land, a place of aversion and "no-saying" without the corresponding "yes," the assent to reality that contemplation needs. Contemplative seeing and teaching belong on the other side of critical thinking, in the realm of a second-naïveté or "knowing-naïveté," a simplicity and wholeheartedness that transcends cynicism. Otherwise, the *method* of critical thinking can turn into a *metaphysics* of nihilism, a sociology of cynicism, and a psychology of pessimism, culminating in an ethics of relativism. We unwittingly collude in the student's wearing of the mask of cynicism when all we offer is doubt. If the method does not open us to the great ideas and connect us to the larger reality of infinite mystery, whether in the sciences or in humanities, we sentence ourselves and our students to a self-constructed prison, to "mind-forged manacles," in Blake's phrase, unable to look upon the stars. A reflective knowing that includes—but transcends—criticism prepares us for the receptivity of contemplation.

It is not the abyss of doubt we want to sink students into for good. I remember one job interview, at a small Catholic college no less, where the faculty told me they felt their ultimate purpose in teaching was to disabuse students of their childhood faith—period. After that comment, I did not want the job. Unlike some postmodernists who seem to want to sweep away truth—meaning God, the self, and the subject—we can say as boldly as Meister Eckhart, "I pray to God that he may make me free of 'God,'"[23] meaning that we are seeking a deeper truth and more authentic relation to self and to God than mere formulas. For Eckhart as well as other medieval mystics, the "unknowing of God"—clearing out the images and words—was as necessary as knowing God. Questions like "Where was God in the Holocaust?" and "How does God create in an evolving universe?" may lead beyond doubt to new insights about the nature of God. Another quite painful question for students is what were Christian attitudes toward Jews through most of Christian history? We can understand this emptying even of our most sacred categories, then, as a religious version of the clearing-out process that postmodern critics advocate. We can make this purgation religiously, guided by the Spirit, or simply enter the void.

Students seem to want to reflect when given the opportunity and the right conditions. Like many other teachers, I have found that *writing*—in journals, short response papers, and computer conversations where students engage with each other throughout the course—constitutes a powerful tool of reflection. Students' own reflections on reflection are helpful. As one student wrote in his journal, "writing and reflecting is a tool by which we become one with emotion and our souls," and, "Reflection equals 'life squared.' Life becomes more meaningful." Another comments, "The Merton presentations, to say the least, made us realize only the self can make something happen....And once we trust us, and are committed to us, we are able to seek contemplation, silence, and reflection." A random selection from a set of unclaimed student journals that have sat in my office for several years includes these comments: "I always think things will be the same as when I put them in my diary, happy or sad. So I write to remind myself how quickly they change and how things rarely are as bad as they seem then." This comment enables me to see that in this student, reflection, like meditation, serves to overcome depression and stress. After reading Merton's essay, "Learning to Live," about the purpose of education as self-discovery, another student says, "I wonder if Merton would agree that as students we are to make time for contemplation…There have been numerous times I have had to take walks around campus just to settle my thoughts and emotions. In these times of distress, I have been able to ask myself, 'Who am I?' and 'Why am I at [this school]?' The answers to these questions continually change as I discover more about myself."

The chronicling of change, of growth in self-reflection, is a miraculous product of the journaling process. When one student, who used the journal mostly to disagree, came to Annie Dillard's writings, she wrote, "I think if everyone could see as Dillard does…people would realize how everything around them is rich with life." In the same entry, she wrote about "discovering small truths and adding them up to greater and greater truths until you go beyond that in search of universal truths as the contemplative does." The technological form of journal, in computer conversations and chat rooms, multiplies reflection exponentially, keeping multiple threads open for discussion as a course moves along. During the build-up to war in Iraq in 2003, a thread I called "Reflections in a Time of War" received multiple postings as students checked in with each other and gave vent to their feelings and thoughts in such a polarizing time. As the bombing began, a whole class period devoted to students' writing, along with reflection on Denise Levertov's poem "Making Peace," produced some fine offerings, including these words from a poem written in class:

Sadd, am I
wishing that worlds weren't
–split–

between Ones
of right, and
of wrong.
And bombs drop on Baghdad,
my books heavy, burden–
indifferent deliverance
of peace.[24]

I am always amazed and humbled by the quality and abundance of insight released by times of reflection and meditation in the classroom. It is truly the "hundredfold."

Teachers' Wells

As a learner, and now a teacher, I have had to clear out my own well often. One of the greatest problems I had in graduate school was mental clutter. As I worked through one philosophical system after another, I felt as if the inner springs that used to flow freely and cleanly had become clogged with the litter of discarded ideas. My well had become a garbage dump. At the suggestion of a friend, a former contemplative nun, I got away to a monastery by the sea for a few days. There, in quiet time alone and in attending the Liturgy of the Hours in choir with the sisters, I sensed that all of life in the monastery was saturated with meaning, backlit by multiple "reflections" from the praying of the psalms. When I simply sat down in the quiet of my room and took up a notebook, I felt more attuned to the "mystery of my being" than I had for years. The singing on the outside began to occur in my soul. When I do meditation now, especially when I go away on retreat, I feel that I am clearing away the debris to open the wellhead again.

Reflection as Mirroring: Relatedness

Reflection refers to the bending back and turning around from various angles that a mirror, or with more suppleness, a pool of water—does to its object. Marguerite Porete's *Mirror for Simple Souls* depicts the soul as a mirror infinitely reflecting the love of God. The mirror was for her a symbol of wholeness and simplicity.[25] To the extent that our reflection approaches the emptiness of actual meditation, to that extent does our mind become clear like a bell, a lake, or a mirror. Mystics and contemplatives throughout the ages have been especially fond of these watery metaphors of still, clear mirroring. Next to fire (an image of transformation), water and mirrors predominate as symbols of clarity, nakedness, and transparency before God.

Mirroring Students

Like the well which must be cleared so the mirror can faithfully reflect its subjects, it must itself become clear and empty.[26] Like the parent, the teacher's most important reflective task consists of reflecting back the true self of the student. We reflect our students when we shine their own light back to them, letting them know they are their own light-source. The teacher's purpose is "to illumine, rather than to shine," as Thomas Aquinas says. If the mirror is either too shiny or too clouded with self-preoccupation, the student cannot see herself and begin her own task of reflection. The myth of Narcissus warns that when the mind is not still, but busily self-absorbed, when otherness within and without is refused, a narcissistic self-love—not relatedness, not depth, not transcendence—ensues. Otherwise, "we literally screen out 'noise' that doesn't fit, and we experience the thing before us as it looks when framed with our prescribed theories. In our rush to understand, to know, we at the very least diminish and at the worst brutalize the Other with a gaze that privileges our version of what can, should, ought to be seen before us."[27]

A poem I wrote about my own teacher while on a contemplative retreat demonstrates to me that we can mirror the student's inner well of being.

> Our teacher a mirror, wherein I catch glimpses of the
>   well within Me. The well long covered over with
>   words,
>   Too many words.
> This mirror a door down a hallway I had long
>   forgotten.
> To a place of soul where few take up occupancy any
>   more.
> You know it by the laughter, the soul's glints and
>   gleams,
> Luminous in the pain.

Over the last several years, some teachers at Berea College began engaging in workshops to explore the "inner landscape of teaching." We were making space for reflection on our own teaching, for drawing from the well. One teacher, who happens to teach voice, reflected on the nature of her teaching in these workshops:

> I was the Letterman or Leno of the music history set, but was I really teaching?...I did not want to teach this way ANY MORE! I was not alone with the grief I was experiencing for my class. I wanted to help the students engage with the material with more depth and passion, in other words, with more "heart"...A more dialectical and experiential model would be a better representation of my own identity as a teacher/learner and would also be a truer expression of my own "VOICE" and...the inner voices of the students.[28]

This teacher found it especially ironic that she was a *voice* teacher who yet had to teach "voice" to all her students by letting their hearts as well as their minds engage with the subject of music.

Mirroring the True Self

Reflection is a mirroring of the true self when there is transparency of soul. One question worth asking today—for teachers as well as students—is: How can I continue to reflect my *deepest* self amid the bombardment of media images that tell me what to look like, pundits who tell me what to think, musical lyrics that program my emotions, video games that occupy my leisure, and the many other things that stuff our minds chock full? Reflection in this context simply means checking in with yourself to see if you are still there.

Mirroring Our Subjects

In the monastic tradition of Benedict and Guigo, the page of Scripture had the potential to mirror the self. Metaphorically, the "page" can be whatever subject faces us in this reflective way. Each has a potential to mirror something of ourselves that we may not see alone. When the subjects of our reflection are the great people who have lived, the Gandhis and Martin Luther King Jr.'s and Dorothy Days, then our reflection can lead to mirroring those subjects in our lives. We begin to reflect them as well as reflect on them. I secretly hoped for this kind of reflection in my course on "Communion of Saints," where I introduced students to the writings of Dorothy Day, Thomas Merton, Etty Hillesum, Simone Weil, and others. These courses, I have discovered, create a hall of mirrors, reflecting the student back to himself and leading him out to rethink relationship with others.

At the end of each section of the course, students mirror these "saints" concretely in creating an aesthetic embodiment of a symbol that has emerged in engagement with each author. Embodiments have taken the form of papier mâché trees with hidden symbols (for Hopkins' "God's Grandeur"); foot washings (for Peter Maurin and Dorothy Day); meditations on silence (for Merton); musical collages accompanying interpolations of poetry and biblical readings; and the labeling, numbering, and herding of people that represents something of Etty Hillesum's dehumanizing experiences in the Holocaust. These aesthetic creations embody interior reflection.

Reflection on Mystery: Transcendence

In a contemplative style of teaching, our reflection, open to possibilities in all directions, can open onto the transcendence of mystery. The point of a contemplative reflection that is not stuck in its own reasoning is to see God and to see the self and world that God sees. The great mystery of reflection occurs when, in seeing ourselves in our depths, we see the other in relation; in seeing the other, we see God. We have spoken of the teacher as mirror, but this image provides only a partial truth. Ultimately, each of us, teacher and student, is a mystery that we come up against in our encounters with one another. The mirror can remind us of the well inside each of us, but it cannot transgress it. Even though each of us has our own well that is the source of our uniqueness, as we learn to draw from the wisdom of our own wells we encounter more universality, perhaps because each well is watered from one underground stream, like the waters of Siloe beneath Jerusalem. Our Carthusian writer's final words on the function of meditation make a fitting commentary on the practice of reflection as transcendence: "[God] gives words to many, but to few that wisdom of the soul which the

Lord apportions to whom He pleases and when He pleases."[29] Wisdom, the fruit of contemplative reflection, is a gift that is meant to be shared. In allowing our wells to be watered from the underground springs, as from Teresa's second trough, we open to mystery.

Contemplative knowing reflects on and engages with the mystery of things; it moves from "small truths" to "greater and greater truths." As Albert Einstein has said, "the most beautiful experience we can have is the mysterious. It is the fundamental emotion which stands at the cradle of true art and true science....I am satisfied with the mystery of the eternity of life and with the awareness and a glimpse of the marvelous structure of the existing world, together with the devoted striving to comprehend a portion...of the Reason that manifests itself in nature."[30] When reflection dares to confront mystery, it opens to transcendence. If I were ever asked to enumerate the mysteries of life, I would list at least these three: the mystery of being, and those in the sciences know this mystery or at least skirt it and flirt with it; the mystery of being able to reflect on being, and those of us in the humanities, psychology, and the social sciences dwell there, whether we acknowledge it or not; and a third mystery—that being, and reflective knowing of being, come together in ways that we still cannot account for.

In this last and most elusive of all mysteries—that our minds can know the world, that as Einstein says, "reason manifests in nature"—the mystery that engages us most in the classroom, contemplation occurs. St. Thomas was right...to teach is *tradere contemplativa:* "to share the fruits of contemplation." To see our knowing as contemplative reflection is to see that we encounter one or more of the faces of mystery—its beauty, its truth, its goodness—in everything we know. A many-faceted diamond, the mystery merits reflection of all its faces. We reflect on the mystery of goodness in the great people who have lived, as Philip Hallie found in the people of Le Chambon, the village in southern France where Christians sheltered Jews from the Nazis during the Holocaust.[31] Attention first catches the mystery under its face of beauty, while reflection reflects (literally) its face of truth and goodness. These are the "things" worth knowing. Being contemplative knowers changes how we know; it changes what we see; and finally it changes who we are in the process. When we become contemplative knowers, we become lovers of the beauty, goodness, and truth at the heart of things.

In the realm of mystery, where the mind's control breaks down, a deeper reflection is the only way through. Reflection particularly needs hope to guide it through and beyond the impasses of thought and existence. We learn to walk again the fine line between expectation and hopelessness. That "line" actually opens into the expansive space called "hope." Falling over the line into expectation means succumbing to the restless desires and fantasies that trap one in the future; falling the other way means shutting down in despair. Hope, not expectation, exists where no prescribed outcome is certain and predictable, but the process itself is seen as worthwhile and ennobling. We *teach* hope and witness to it by our very presence as contemplative teachers. The theological virtues of faith, hope, and love guide each step of *lectio divina*. Just as there is something of faith in attention, there needs to be something of hope in reflection, and of love in receptivity. Marguerite Porete's *Mirror for Simple Souls* staged a dialogue where Reason dies in its debate with Love. This last subject we take up in the next chapter.

Some Concrete Proposals for Reflection

- Place fewer subjects before students and allow them to go deeper into each one.
- Make time for "ah-ha" papers, papers that capture a moment of realization or shift in perception, "minute" papers, with time for queries such as "What is the most important lesson I have learned today?" and "What questions remain?"
- Journal along with your students.
- Create sacred time through ritual and silence.
- Contemplate a poem in relation to your subject.

CHAPTER 4

Receptivity

> I kiss my hand
> To the stars, lovely-asunder
> Starlight, wafting him out of it; and
> Glow, glory in thunder;
> Kiss my hand to the dappled-with-damson west:
> Since, tho' he is under the world's splendour and wonder,
> his mystery must be instressed, stressed:
> For I greet him the days I meet him, and bless when I
> understand.
> —Gerard Manley Hopkins, from
> "The Wreck of the Deutschland"

Climbing Guigo's ladder of contemplative learning, or dancing out the steps, we have come from the *lectio* of attention to the *meditatio* of reflection, and are now ready for the *oratio* of prayer. If faith is the chief theological virtue of attention, and hope of reflection, then love is the virtue of *oratio*. "Love" is understood here as a rediscovered ontological connection—a connection that is already there—rather than a romantic excess of feeling or a moralistic act of will. Love, as fundamental connection, has been present at all the stages and in each of the practices of a contemplative mode of teaching, or we would not be at this stage at all. Love has engendered *lectio,* the desire to look beyond oneself and one's projections to the other, and *meditatio,* the deep concentration on the meaning and mystery at the heart of things. When love is present, the heart is ready to open, meaning we are ready for the receptivity that leads to transformation in learning.

Prayer in Teaching: Receptivity

If *lectio* is simple awareness *that* you are there, and if *meditatio* is reflection on *what* you are, then *oratio,* prayer, is the beginning of I-Thou relation. As "I-Thou" speech, prayer invokes the tender, undefended core of each person's "I" in relation to the other/Other. Without a dialogue that addresses the "Thou," whether subject or student, education cannot be "I-Thou" speech, that is, *prayerful.* In attention, we have privileged the other, and in reflection we have privileged the "I" capable of addressing a "Thou." In the receptivity of prayer, we turn to the other as "Thou" from the depths of our ability to say "I." Our receptivity helps turn a teacher's I-It relationships with students or a student's with subjects—those that objectify them and put them at a distance—into I-Thou relationships. Without the "I-Thou" of receptive prayer, we would bounce between the polarities of the ego and the other, disallowing one or the other. We could neither be "I" nor say "Thou." The I-Thou nature of prayer opens the self to reception of the other.

So crucial is the personal I and Thou to prayer that when our Carthusian guide, Guigo, speaks of prayer he departs from his usual third-person commentary to frame this element in the I-Thou language of prayer itself:

> Lord, for long have I meditated in my heart, seeking to see your face. It is the sight of you, Lord, that I have

sought; and all the while in my meditation the fire of longing, the desire to know you more fully, has increased. *When you break for me the bread of sacred Scripture,* you have shown yourself to me in that breaking of bread.[1] (italics added)

For Guigo, prayer helps not only to *see* the God we have sought in meditation, but to make us literally *companions,* those who break bread with the Lord. And the implication follows that in prayer, the Lord, who has disguised himself through the earlier encounters of *lectio* and *meditatio,* will reveal himself "in the breaking of bread," as he did to his disciples after the resurrection. For those of us who labor and teach outside the monastery, if *meditatio* can lead us into the dark night of God's absence, and into the death of reason in its encounter with the impasses of existence, prayer as receptivity can open us to glimpses of the dawn, to the Lord here in our midst. As Parker Palmer has put it, "If study forms me in images of love, prayer opens me to receive a love that is beyond imaging; it forms me in that receptiveness to love that is at the heart of the spiritual journey."[2]

Dom Jean LeClercq, himself a monk and scholar of monasticism, once told a class at St. John's Abbey that when we celebrate the gift of existence, we are praying. "I pray, therefore I exist," he said. On this view, whenever we accept ourselves in the presence of ultimate mystery, that is prayer. The autobiographical move, begun in reflection that is self-reflective, is an inherently spiritual one, a move in the direction of the I-Thou language necessary for prayer. I venture my self, and I speak my self. In prayer, the silence of deep reflection and authentic speech exist in paradoxical relation.

Prayer, the spontaneous movement of the heart in response to God's initiative, unites us to ourselves, to God, and to the world. For many people, prayer is private, and almost always about asking for things.[3] But prayer is, as Parker Palmer so aptly calls it, the "practice of relatedness."[4] And it is also receptivity. The English word *prayer* means petition or request,[5] implying that in prayer we stand ready to receive. We receive our own true self, a self hidden behind the charades of daily life, and we receive the mystery of reality. Prayer includes all three aspects of spiritual practice in their most refined form: prayer brings us to our own *depths,* where "the Spirit intercedes for us with sighs too deep for words" (Rom 8:26); it *relates* us to the world from a place outside our egos; and finally, prayer opens our hearts to the *transcendent Other* in our midst. When C. S. Lewis asked, "How can [the gods] meet us face to face till we have faces?"[6] he was putting forward the necessity of presenting our real faces to God. The transcendence of prayer is the Spirit's immanence in us, invoked by our willingness to show our true face, and to be called by our own name.

Natural self-defenses and self-protectiveness make this stage both difficult and critical, a turning point into the contemplative way. If teaching and learning reach this third stage, the stage of the *heart,* they become truly contemplative and integrative because only the heart can mediate between the body and the mind. Only the heart can bring together the sense perceptions of attention, and the cognitive energies of reflection. Even though we can give reading and reflection a somewhat spiritual cast, they can get along perfectly well as secular endeavors. But with receptivity, education and spirituality, which had been on parallel tracks, begin to converge. Colleges and schools hold many receptions, while not necessarily being places that cultivate receptivity. Receptivity opens up a channel of compassion: we receive and cross over to the other in a constant, fluid exchange. At this stage of *lectio divina,* we come to realize that education and the life of the spirit have the same goal:

to cultivate compassion and integrity. With receptivity, teaching becomes the practice of compassion and hospitality.

Lectio, or reading by itself (the constant discipline of surveying our fields, even if it awakens us to the world), and *meditatio,* or reflection by itself (the careful study and weighing of evidence and reasons) even if it is reflection on mystery, will not transform us without the dimensions of *oratio,* that engagement of the heart that leads to the lover's union with what is known and seen. "The good and the wicked alike can read and meditate and even pagan philosophers by the use of reason discovered the highest and truest good," said Guigo in the thirteenth century.[7] Even if we are attentive and reflective in learning, no deep learning—no wisdom—will occur unless we open our hearts. Intellectual impasses can lead either to despair and hopelessness or to the heart and its love. On a retreat a few years ago, I heard the retreat master say, "You are more than your thoughts; you are more than your stories," and at that moment I felt my heart open after a lifetime of over-identifying with my thinking self. These first two stages lead the learner to transformation through the entryway of receptivity.

Guigo's Journey toward the Heart

Deep learning is really about change of heart, what Jesus called *metanoia.* Often translated to mean "repentance," *metanoia* also means breaking open your heart or having it broken, transcending your ordinary view of reality. *Metanoia* is the way out of impasse. This kind of learning may happen only a few times in our lifetime, where we are utterly converted to a new way of seeing and of being. Albert Schweitzer may have had such a paradigm shift when he gave up his intellectual career—trying to figure out who the historical Jesus really was, an attempt that ended in an impasse—and went on to found a hospital for lepers in the heart of equatorial Africa. We may finally realize the plight of the poor, the suffering of those addicted to drugs or alcohol, and the subordinate place of women.

The heart of contemplative knowing and learning is actually the heart. Guigo expresses the incompleteness of *meditatio* without this third stage in these words:

> But what is [meditation] to do? It is consumed with longing, yet it can find no means of its own to have what it longs for; and the more it searches the more it thirsts. As long as it is meditating, so long is it suffering because it does not feel that same sweetness which, as meditation shows, belongs to purity of heart, but which it does not give.[8]

Suffering, brought on by the unattainability of its desire, actually helps break open the heart. This "broken heart" with its woundedness is the very beginning of receptivity. We have gotten to this place of heart through a reflectiveness willing to engage and risk the self in its reflection. *Lectio divina* now becomes a "journey toward the heart."

Prayer begins when we can say "taste and see" of the texts we have "eaten" and "chewed," texts encountered in sacred reading and reflected on. Guigo's food metaphor involves a process of nourishment that feeds and integrates the whole person. But Guigo goes further. In his *Meditations*, Guigo uses the same language to describe the reception of the word as the reception of the Eucharist, making them implicitly kindred:

> This is what it means to eat the body of Christ spiritually: to have pure faith in Him, and carefully meditating upon that same faith, always to seek, and understanding what we seek, to find, and *ardently to love what we find,* and to imitate as much as we can what we

love,...and clinging to Him, to be made one with Him for all eternity.[9] (italics added)

Guigo uses gustatory metaphors to emphasize the very deep embedding that the whole process of *lectio divina* effects.[10]

Teaching as Communion

As Merton said right before he died: "The deepest level of communication is not communication but communion. It is wordless....Not that we discover a new unity. We discover an older unity. My dear brothers, we are already one. But we imagine that we are not. And what we have to recover is our original unity."[11] Although it may sound radical to say it, in contemplative teaching what we are educating for is not freedom alone, the freedom we may find if we stop with reflection, but this deep communion with others. Martin Buber speaks of communion as the end of education:

> Freedom in education is the possibility of *communion*...it is the run before the jump, the tuning of the violin, the confirmation of that primal and mighty potentiality which it cannot even begin to actualize.[12]

Just getting our students to become freethinkers is a great leap forward, but not the end of the jump. If reflection establishes our freedom from the herd mentality, then receptivity uses that freedom positively—for communion. If we are going to make that leap of connection, or play that polyphonic music of harmony, we need more than the run up to it or the tuning of our instruments. By analogy, then, encountering the word (or world) through attention, seeking and meditating on it in reflection, then receiving and loving what we seek is a sacramental act, an act of holy communion. If our teaching does these things, it becomes sacramental.

One educational theorist, David Kolb, has given educators a four-stage theory of the learning cycle, which oddly corresponds to much of Guigo's ladder with one significant exception.[13] The first stage of Kolb's inventory of learning styles involves concrete experience; the second, reflection; the third, abstract conceptualization; and the last, practical application. Kolb's learning styles inventory has opened up tremendous opportunities to see how students learn in different ways and for teachers to "teach around the circle." When I first encountered it in a teaching seminar for new faculty, I was excited by the opportunities it presented to teach around the circle of differing learning styles. The correspondences between Kolb's Jungian-based model and Guigo's monastic model are remarkable. But the principal difference is equally instructive: where Kolb's third stage offers "abstract conceptualization," literally a "drawing away from" and crystallizing of reflective observation and concrete experience, the *oratio* of Guigo's ladder brings us to the heart. From the perspective of contemplative learning, the third stage of this scheme almost looks like a heart bypass.

Instead of conceptualization, *oratio* is "conception," a receiving and conceiving of the other within the womb of self. This is another way of saying that unconscious, nonrational processes are at work in receptivity. Conception entails a long period of growth in darkness, a nurturing in the fertile dark until the new idea, new life, is ready for the light. Like a mother-to-be rejoicing over news of her pregnancy, it welcomes and makes a place for the other in the home of the heart. We find ourselves more willing to entertain an idea rather than usher it out with a dismissive judgment. In order to bring "home" the experiences we encounter concretely, the thoughts we reflect on, the ideas we conceptualize, and the people we meet, what we need is a renewed sense of hospitality in teaching. Because we spend so much of our lives learning how *not* to be receptive and vulnerable to new ideas and to strangers, especially in this era of terror threats and color-coded alerts, acknowledging the other proves a tremendously difficult task; it is almost a death. Perhaps that explains why the practice of hospitality has virtually disappeared from our culture and why the symbols of defensiveness—guns—have replaced it. As Joan Chittister construes it, "Only the contemplative lives well in a world the security of which depends on the open heart."[14]

Benedict's Hospitality

Hospitality was central to St. Benedict's *Rule*. He devoted a long chapter to it, instructing his monks that "All guests to the monastery should be welcomed as Christ."[15] Benedict based this rule on the text of Matthew's Gospel, "I was a stranger, and you took me in" (Matt 25:35), although he could also have been familiar with the Old Testament's frequent command not to oppress a resident alien (e.g., Exod 22:20). Monks are to greet the guest with love and "great humility," demonstrated in gestures of a bow and prostration. Then they are to pray together with him and give him the kiss of peace. In effect, Benedict offers a liturgy of hospitality for welcoming strangers: (1) greeting with prostrations, (2) praying together, and (3) giving the kiss of peace. In these steps lies a prescription for a hospitable kind of contemplative learning. We greet others in giving our attention, sometimes even having to bow a little; we "pray together" in reflection and give them the kiss of peace in receptivity. The point of Benedictine hospitality is to greet and bless *everyone* as Christ. A single line from Gerard Manley Hopkins' poem, "The Wreck of the Deutschland," encompasses these three movements: "For I *greet* him the days I *meet* him, and *bless* when I *understand*"[16] (italics added). What might these steps mean to a contemplative teaching style?

Hospitable Teaching

In order to talk about the receptivity of contemplative teaching we need some new metaphors. Perhaps in part because the feminist revolution has changed all our categories, time and its linear paradigms are giving way to the paradigm of space as an alternative vision. Now that time is bending back on itself, in the new physics at least, space appears as paradigmatic. In his book, *Reaching Out*, Henri Nouwen views the practice of teaching through the metaphors of hospitality and the creation of hospitable space. "When we look at teaching in terms of hospitality," he says, "we can say that the teacher is called upon to create for [her] students a free and fearless space where mental and emotional development can take place." Hospitable space is safe space. In such a hospitable space, "people are encouraged to disarm themselves, to lay aside their occupations and preoccupations and to listen with attention and care to the voices speaking in their own center."[17] To listen with attention is the first step of a contemplative teaching style. Who is speaking, and who is the "I" who hears?

It is no accident that the metaphor of hospitality fits this stage of learning. For it is here, in opening the heart, that learning comes "home." We not only welcome strangers to our classrooms and to the home of our heart; we ourselves come home. Someone needs to be at home for our students to feel welcome. The metaphor of home could be seen as complementary to the more prominent journey metaphor in spirituality today. In adopting it for this stage of learning, we may be giving up to some extent the sense of touristy adventure, of "if it's Tuesday, it must be Paris," or Islam, or the sixteenth century, or spermatozoa. But what we gain is a sense of belonging, of stability, of place.

Greetings and Prostrations

Recognizing the need to overcome differences between the vulnerability of the guests and the relative security of their hosts, Benedict greeted his guests with a bow: "All humility should be shown in addressing a guest on arrival or departure. By a bow of the head or by a complete prostration of the body, Christ is to be adored and welcomed in them."[18] Some similarities exist between the wandering pilgrims of Benedict's day and our itinerant students. Like his medieval guests, coming in for shelter and nurture from the outside world's dangers, our students make themselves vulnerable just by showing up in our classrooms. Benedict also notices class distinctions among guests: "Special care," says Benedict, "should be taken of the poor and pilgrims, for Christ is truly made welcome in them: wealth creates its own impression."[19] Though our students might outclass us in wealth, our relationship with them is not a symmetrical or reciprocal one: we teachers possess more power and security in the situation, making our students decidedly "second-class" in the politics of the classroom. Students, painfully conscious of this asymmetry, may try to equalize it in their own way.

When the "I" metaphorically bows to the other, the arrogant, exaggerated ego, whose performance threatens to steal the show, must give way. Jane Tompkins made such a metaphorical bow when she realized that teaching could be more than performance:

> I remember walking down the empty hall to class (always a little bit late) and thinking to myself, "I have to remember to find out what they want, what they need, and not worry about whether what I've prepared is good enough or ever gets said at all."...I

had been putting on a performance whose true goal was not to help the students learn but to perform before them in such a way that they would have a good opinion of me.[20]

What a tremendous act of prostration of self this shift in perspective entailed. Gestures of true humility in greeting the other neutralize the power differential undermining teacher-student relations. Ideally, a good teacher, like a good host, is receptive to these "poor pilgrims"—receiving their gifts and promises and enabling them to become receptive in turn.

Teaching becomes hospitable when both the "I" and the "Thou" are acknowledged with a gesture like Benedict's bow and prostration.[21] Students may exact some form of prostration from us whether we intend it or not. As I completed a historical-critical exegesis of a biblical text one day, a student exclaimed, "But that's just your opinion." Perhaps mindful of 2 Timothy 2:12, "I permit no woman to teach," I had been unconsciously trying to assert my authority by standing in front of the class; after that, I sat in a circle with them, and this neutralizing of my authority, at least in a physical way, seemed to relax the class a bit more. I had not made a conscious or unconscious bow to their status as uneasy newcomers to the inner circle of textual criticism.

Sometimes students poke holes in our teacherly personas, as when a student asked me—just when I was explaining what stages of faith *they* were going through—to tell *my* story. Trained as I am in the academic study of religion, which by definition leaves out the "I," I find myself more challenged than most to bring it back. I could either remain behind my shield of objective knowledge or let it drop to reveal a tender place in myself. One day, when a student challenged me to reveal my story of faith and doubt, I halted, and awkwardly began talking of my own struggles with doubt, and of the courage I have learned from my father who once was a prisoner in Buchenwald concentration camp and yet had a faith in life and a deep commitment to the good. I had to make not only a bow but a prostration. I spoke of how I was trying to understand and forgive God for what had happened to my father and all the others during the Holocaust. The student later remarked, "That made you a real person, someone we can connect to." For students, my inability to understand God's ways was more real than my careful reasoning. I may have connected with pain they have experienced from drugs, broken relationships, abuse, or lack of parenting. Still, I chose to reveal this aspect of my spiritual autobiography and to withhold others. Although I might not have wanted to tell this story in just this way or at this point, the "I" coaxed out of me is essential to the I who can learn to become "prayerful" in the classroom.

Hospitality requires that an "I" coming to know itself must exist on both sides of the desk. The absence of the "I" willing to risk itself prevents both teachers and students from telling their own stories. When either the student's "I" or the teacher's cannot emerge, the danger of monologism, of talking to oneself, exists. If the student or the teacher "disappears," or if the subject is completely "mastered" (notice the hierarchical, patriarchal language), relationship becomes impossible. The indispensable *and* in the "I *and* Thou" constitutes the *contemplative* way of seeing the other as other without losing the connection. This little conjunction does not subordinate either I or Thou, initiating an either-or rejection of one for the other. Hospitality is the practice of the *and*.

Guests and Safe Space

Some guests make a space even more hospitable. Students, unpredictable and resistant as they can be, make us better hosts, that is, better teachers. In a commentary on monastic wisdom called "Xenophilia: The Love of Strangers," Joan Chittister speaks of what this means to a contemplative:

> There are few things in life more threatening to the person whose religion is parochialism than the alien and few things more revelatory to the contemplative than the stranger....It is the stranger who disarms all our preconceptions about life and penetrates all our stereotypes about the world. It is the stranger who makes the supernatural natural. It is the stranger who tests all our good intentions.[22]

Strangers indeed, if not at times aliens to us who can be so parochial, our students constantly test and reform us in our good intentions. That is teaching. What Joan Chittister says of receiving all guests applies especially to our students:

> Our role in life is not to convert others. It's not even to influence them. It certainly is not to impress them. Our goal in life is to convert ourselves from the pernicious agenda that is the self to an awareness of God's goodness present in the other."[23]

Hospitality in the context of teaching might mean acknowledging the goodness of the students, breaking bread with them, or inviting them into the "rule" that will enable them to shed their unruliness for the discipline of the house. In all three of these gestures, we implicitly acknowledge that Christ is present in the "least of these" (Matt 25:40).

Guests Who Don't Stay Put

Poetry, stories, and silence make great guests, allowing for a safe and hospitable space. Contemplative space is receptive to poetry and to all the arts, with their metaphoric process that itself enacts transformation. As metaphor carries us across from the known to the unknown, as in the classroom experience of building on what we know and leaning into what we do not know, it weaves a pattern of interconnectedness among the things of this life and their inherent mystery. The metaphorical nature of poetry reminds us that neither the univocal speech of the absolutely certain—saying it only this way and no other—nor the equivocal speech of the relativists and nihilists—saying there is no meaning—has the most fruitful word. The word that bears most fruit stands in the middle, inviting fundamentalists and secularists as well into the middle ground of metaphor and paradox. A poem makes a grand affirmation that not all the answers are in, that mystery abounds, and we are on the edge of it all the time. The space around the poem, the pauses within, form silent testimonies to a greatness we have yet to grasp. Poetry's purpose is to bear witness. Its witness, constituting an affirmation of the world in its beauty and its pain, makes for a great guest.

Stories also make a space more hospitable to contemplative learning, connecting us to the human story. Storytelling is perhaps the child's most excellent means of trying on new possibilities for her life. Stories have a way of "getting in" where abstractions cannot. The call of stories is, as one of Robert Coles's students put it, that they are the word made flesh in us.

> The whole point of stories is not "solutions" or "resolutions" but a broadening and even a heightening of our struggles—with new protagonists and antagonists introduced, with new sources of concern or apprehension or hope, as one's mental life accommodates itself to a series of arrivals: guests who have a way of staying, but not necessarily staying put.[24]

Stories invite a series of "others" who slip in unannounced, and who often turn out to be provocative guests.

Putting this metaphor of story as guest into practice in the sciences could mean using the method of case study, where we could walk around "inside" the case, making ourselves at home in it. The Web site on Case Studies in Science at the University of Buffalo states that the use of case studies "humanizes science." One teacher who has incorporated this method writes: "I used to worry about content in my classes, about how I could cram so much of the textbook into my lectures. I still teach a lot of material, but I don't worry about getting through it all."[25] Case studies are essentially *stories* that students can inhabit in ways the lecture method does not allow. They let students in and they get into them.

Another guest, *silence*, can create hospitality, though it may bring awkwardness in the door with it. When we invite silence into the learning space, we send a signal that we want our students to reach for their authentic selves, not just to impress or please us. In a course on the History of Western Civilization, a Great Books course, a composition course, and a survey of Western civilization all rolled into one—a course with no extra time, in other words—I gave *five minutes* of silence and meditation at the beginning of class one day. This brief assignment, not carried out with any particular finesse on my part, prompted reflective responses from my students who spoke of feeling "peace," "getting a perspective on life," "leaving the usual chaos," "hearing the birds for the first time all semester," "experiencing a sense of oneness with nature," "hearing a running stream that became still," and "feeling safe." They received this silence as a guest bearing them important gifts.

Strangers Rather Than Aliens

In his description of teaching as hospitality, Nouwen explains that true receptivity means inviting strangers into our world on their terms, without imposing our religious or ideological viewpoint on them. The diversity and pluralism of our world today pose a great challenge to our hospitality. An African-American female student who grew up in the projects of Louisville told a group of us faculty some years ago, "diversity is not enough without some way of speaking across our differences." I heard her message, and so I resolved to begin an interfaith dialogue program, where students of different faith traditions come together, often for a meal, to learn about each other's traditions, but to learn hospitality as well. In contrast to the dominant culture, where xenophobia seems to reign, and fear of Muslims joins fear of immigrants from other regions, in interfaith dialogue the stranger is welcomed. In the face-to-face encounter of the dialogue, we continually learn to break down our categories, caricatures, and even our theologies of the other.

The most transformative aspect of this program has been our table fellowship with each other, our breaking bread with each other in face-to-face conversation. The hidden "Christ" keeps emerging, from the Tibetan Buddhist student who has shared his singing bowl for meditation with us, to the Muslim women who proudly wear their *shadurs* as badges of dignity and the Muslim men who tell stories of Islam in their various cultures, to the Christians who respectfully listen instead of having the answers, to the layman in the Hindu temple who speaks of using gods like "walkers" until we are mature enough to walk without them, that is, to know God without forms. They are all great guests with so much to teach us.

One year a group of us, Muslims and Buddhists and Christians, visited the Cistercian Abbey of Gethsemane where we saw on the entrance wall to the guesthouse Benedict's words, "Let all guests be received as Christ." A Muslim student remarked that she loved that saying, recalling from her own tradition of the Qur'an the saying, "Which of the favors of the Lord will you refuse today?" Interfaith and intrafaith dialogue can happen in the classroom if we can take off some of our armor, our own sense of rightness and our prejudgments of the other. Our dialogue is then not only a "logos between two" (literally "dialogue") but a "conversation," a turning together.

Troublesome Guests

Sometimes both guests and hosts have to be a bit troublesome to perform their roles well. Some sort of "disorienting dilemma"[26] or "disconfirming other"[27] is essential to initiate the process of transformation at the heart of real learning. The disorienting dilemma can come not only with the stranger in our midst but in the guise of a book or story (e.g., a Scripture from another tradition), poem, piece of art, or cultural experience that disconfirms our prior assumptions about what is true and valuable.[28] Or it can be the last person we would want in this room, recalling Parker Palmer's understanding of community as the place where the person we least want to interact with resides. The human tendency to exclude, to keep out the "undesirables," must be patiently overcome by practices of inclusion and hospitality.

One could read the gospels as a series of disorienting, disconfirming encounters. Jesus was adept at this fellowship of inclusion of the excluded ones, of inviting people in to table who did not belong, and of encounters that shook up the status quo. Jesus punctured the Pharisees' cult mentality, their willingness to have table fellowship only among one another, and to leave out women, *am ha'aretz* (common people), sinners, and misfits. He exposed them right where they were most sure of themselves and most proud. Prostitutes, on both counts of being sinners and women, were extremely "disconfirming" to the Pharisees' worldview. But just in case his own followers could start feeling "pharisaical" about their own openness to others, Jesus did the same to them when they argued over whether a woman with a jar of spike-nard was welcome. Similarly, Jews became disconfirming throughout the Middle Ages to ordinary Christians, with the result that attempts to reduce their irreducibility by conversion and expulsion ended with annihilation during the Holocaust.

But what happens when we have to invite in those things toward which we do not wish to be hospitable? How do we invite the evil of the Holocaust into our classrooms, for example? As the child of a Holocaust survivor, I feel especially vulnerable to this question. Do we invite this subject in so that we can treat it as a stranger—from *hostes,* that is, with hostility? If it belongs only out there, in Nazi Germany, in profane space, and not in the contemplative space of our classroom, we cannot bring it in to learn from it and be moved by it. We have to realize here that we do not get the luxury of demonizing the Nazis without seeing the evil, the "mote," in our own eyes, that we are the Germans too. The contemplative *and* has to connect us even to this horror. A student who had resisted much of the reading, and argued with me and the class all semester about the need to forgive someone who had done him wrong, could say in a journal:

> I keep telling myself that if Etty [Hillesum] could love her enemies despite all the terrible pain and suffering they inflicted upon her people as well as herself, I need to open my mind and reexamine my beliefs toward love and forgiveness. I always said I could never forgive someone like Hitler for all the needless pain and death he caused, but if Etty could, why can I not?

If we make the Holocaust or any other form of evil an alien, we undo the tremendous power of transformation it can exercise in examining the evil in our own hearts. There can be no *oratio* of the heart and no contemplative receptivity. Its evil remains irreversible, like the evil of the Jews for Hitler. The scapegoating and destruction of one designated group of people, the Jews, belonged to Hitler's logic of the irreversibility of evil. "It is no accident," says Thomas Merton, "that Hitler believed firmly in the unforgivableness of sin." But in the tradition of Christ, "evil is not only reversible but it is the proper motive of that mercy by which it is overcome and changed into good."[29] This ability to take on the suffering and evil of another in order to transform it, rather than banishing the other from our sight or setting out to destroy the "evildoers," belongs to the heart of the Christian gospels, to the Beatitudes, and to the peacemakers, those willing to suffer for justice.

The Hidden Guest

In their compassionate receptivity, teachers are not only hosts to their students, but literally "companions," who break and eat the bread of many communions with their students.[30] In the Emmaus story, Christ revealed himself to the disciples and yet remained somehow elusive. So there is a something "more" in encounters between teachers and students and between students and subjects that we cannot wholly receive and assimilate. This visitor, like the one at Emmaus, is the most elusive of guests, one who never shows up directly. Education becomes "prayerful" when a mysterious third enters this encounter as its horizon as well as its matrix. We could call it "truth" or simply acknowledge our being called by it. Our willingness to respond to its call evokes purity of heart. But we should not give up on expecting it. Benedict's praying together means turning in the direction of a third—the wisdom or truth that has been calling and leading this process from the beginning. As we turn together to the sources of our traditions, and to their Living Source, we come to a turning of our hearts, or *metanoia*.[31] We are challenged to receive the very otherness of the other, and to repent of the ways we as persons and as communities have not loved the other.

Creating Community

If we are lucky, our encounter, conflict, and dialogue (perhaps in that order) will enable the creation of community. Our classrooms have the potential to become communities when our refusal of troublesome guests gives way to a ritual dialogue for embrace of conflict, and we resolve that conflict with a decision to become community. Rosemary Haughton defines community as "the creation of a relationship" that springs from "encounter—a confrontation of the individual by something else, one involving a certain degree of conflict." What Haughton calls Christian community could also be said of the classroom, "an educational structure with room for explosions."[32] If we don't make room for explosions, for conflict, the power to generate transformation dissipates.

Praying Together

The founder of the Benedictine monastic tradition, St. Benedict, instructs his monks to pray with their guest "in order to be at peace."[33] Benedict's *Rule* says that in prayer "God regards our purity of heart and tears of compunction" more than our many words.[34] (He may have learned the value of tears from his sister, Scholastica.) Prayer, then, for Benedict involves these heart qualities: "purity of heart" and "compunction," literally "piercing the heart." This puncturing of the heart opens it to feel its *own* pain, making it possible to receive others in their pain and fragility. This Sufi saying suggests what compunction could mean: "When the heart grieves over what it has lost, the spirit rejoices over what it has found."

Prayer in Disguise

Except for the endless debates about prayer in schools, our schools contain little that could be called "prayer." Many academics find it extremely troubling to connect these two disparate realms in a meaningful way. In what way can we pray with our "guests," our students, in secular schools without running smack-dab into the issues of church-state separation? If the noun *prayer*, as associated with the school setting, has become wholly politicized, the adjective *prayerful* has not fared much better. Parker Palmer's phrase "prayerful education" seems almost an oxymoron. "We cannot settle for pious prayer as a preface to conventional education. Instead, we must allow the power of love to transform the very knowledge we teach, the very methods we use to teach and learn it," Palmer says.[35]

How can we reframe the subject of prayer in order to relate it to teaching? Students may not be receptive to us because of the deep wounding they have experienced in the past and their being "handled" along the way in school. Can we "receive" our students, be a safe space for their emotional baggage, instead of "handling" them?

Oratio, prayer, does not always come neatly packaged in liturgical formulas when it shows up in our classrooms. Prayer may sound like "Oh, my God!" or "Oh Hell" or "I hate this stuff"—more like cries of despair than formal addresses to God. Yet, even these cries announce openings of the heart and point to puncture wounds where the deeper insights of compunction can be born. In just such vulnerable places, receptivity can emerge. We need to learn to listen for the various disguises prayer can take. If our students' "prayers" sound more like Job's angry protests, it helps to remember that Job's honest anger brought him from the "I-It" of a hearsay relationship with God to the beginning of true intimacy. One of my most obstreperous students, who saw his mother killed by a crack addict at the age of four and lived "life on the boundary," spewed out anger one day in protest against a curriculum that excluded his own tradition and culture. Where was Africa? he asked after looking at the map offered in the frontispiece of the text. After the first quiz he announced to the class that he would not read any more of the textbook. His was a cry of the heart, giving voice to his deep woundedness and feelings of exclusion. It was about far more than the curriculum. In his rage, he revealed more of his true self than in listless submissiveness to a curriculum that excluded him. Though I had not wanted his outbursts, he had given me a gift of self as well as an ability to see the course from his point of view. From that point on, I became more questioning of the text myself. He proceeded to give me and the class such a hard time all semester that I was shocked when, a few months later, he came up to me on campus and gave me a hug. In a sense, we had been metaphorically "praying together," which *he* acknowledged with a metaphorical "kiss of peace."

The Kiss of Peace

This last of Benedict's instructions for welcoming a guest may seem the most out of place in a school setting. Yet, if we understand his "kiss of peace" as a metaphorical act of reconciliation, it may be the most needed. "Because of the delusions of the devil," Benedict insisted that only after praying together, only after an opening of the heart, could the abbot and other monks offer the guest the kiss of peace."[36] By "delusions of the devil" he may have meant that we first have to do the work of clearing out the distortions we have about the strangers in our midst. Like the other elements of Benedict's "liturgy," we intend to make this one a metaphor. Our "kisses" of reconciliation could otherwise become psycho-sexual seductions or involve the tendency to do emotional violence to the other. *Delusion* in the Freudian vocabulary means being completely out of touch with reality. If we succeed in removing mutually destructive delusions through praying together, hearing each other's stories and anguish, then learning can become insight. Insight opens up when teaching relies less on a plan or set lecture and more on the working of the Spirit. It happens spontaneously and freely as we become receptive to the Spirit in ourselves and in each other, and to her transcendent illumination.

We need the kiss of peace to restore a unity, a love there from the beginning but lost in the din of competing narratives, "delusions of the devil," and filled-in space. In contemplative teaching, this place is the heart, the place where words give way to silence, ideas to mystery, and the ego to the greater Self.

Peace in Paradox

The irreducible and irreconcilable otherness that remains in teaching creates tensions that necessitate a reconciliation of opposites. Otherwise, these tensions can become debates where someone wins and someone loses, so that we teach domination and submission rather than equality. In contemplative teaching, we *suffer* the tensions and contradictions of our practices—of the I that must both bow to the Other and receive the Other, both embrace conflict and create community through it; the tensions of an attention that focuses on the concrete, of a reflection that must detach from it, of a receptivity that receives and holds them both until we ourselves become paradoxes. We become the paradox of finding our voice by simultaneously listening to the silence within; the paradox of becoming our authentic self by othering ourselves in the big ideas and small acts; the paradox of journeying to the heart to know the other and God more fully. All the so-called "activities" of contemplation then—the listening, the seeing, the attending—involve paradox. In our listening we meet silence; in our seeing, darkness; and in our attending, withdrawal from activity. There we find rest.

Some Concrete Proposals for Receptivity

- Have quiet days at your house where students can drop in.
- Use ritual openings and closings with music and change of lighting.
- Dance.
- Allow learning to be led by desire.
- Use a ritual process to become a contemplative community of learners.

CHAPTER 5

Transformation and Action

For she is a reflection of eternal light,
a spotless mirror of the working of God,
and an image of his goodness.
Although she is but one, she can do all things,
and while remaining in herself, she renews all things;
in every generation she passes into holy souls
and makes them friends of God, and prophets.
—Wisdom of Solomon 7:26–27

Lectio, the act of attention; *meditatio,* the act of reflection; and *oratio,* receptivity to another, have been leading us on this journey of the heart to the final act, which can be called by many names. As we come to the final stage of *lectio divina,* and translate it into classroom practice, we see that all the stages have been present to one another, as Russian dolls one inside the other, or as concentric circles around a center that irradiates them all. Contemplation is a name for the whole process, containing the entire set of practices. Traditionally, *contemplatio* is seeing God, but also being one with God, and there is no place in this circle where that is not possible. In our transmutation into the dynamics of the classroom, contemplation becomes transformation, which names the whole process of attention, reflection, and receptivity. In this final stage we realize a *transformation* into that which we have been contemplating—attending, reflecting, and receiving—that is, the sacredness at the heart of things. Paul provides the paradigmatic statement of this reality: "And all of us, with unveiled faces, seeing the glory of the Lord as though reflected in a mirror, are being transformed into the same image from one degree of glory to another; for this comes from the Lord, the Spirit" (2 Cor 3:18). The mirrors of "the glory of the Lord" are everywhere, or as Meister Eckhart puts it, "When the Son is born in the soul, God shines out of every creature." Paul's extremely hopeful declaration avows that the creation's reflections of God's "glory" (God's shining presence in the world) can transform us. The fourteenth-century Flemish mystic, Jan van Ruysbroeck, echoed him when he said, "We become what we behold; we behold what we are." If we want full, complete human beings in the teaching endeavor, our attending, reflecting, and receiving must both form us and *transform* us. Transformation has been going on in all the *formative* stages that have come before, but now it breaks out, as it were. Transformation is the *teleos* of Jesus' "Be perfect [complete], as your heavenly Father is perfect" (Matt 5:48).

For Guigo and the entire contemplative tradition, contemplation is not only the goal, but the means as well. Guigo offers a summary of the way each stage anticipates and involves the others:

> Reading comes first, and is, as it were, the foundation; it provides the subject matter we must use for meditation. Meditation considers more carefully what is to be sought after....Prayer lifts itself up to God with all its strength, and begs for the treasure it longs for, which is the sweetness of contemplation. Contemplation when it

comes rewards the labors of the other three; it inebriates the thirsting soul with the dew of heavenly sweetness.[1]

The stages of *lectio divina* can be likened to colors of the rainbow overlapping, ebbing, and flowing into one another.[2] By closing the circle or filling in the rainbow, we do a sacred reading of the whole of life. The Holy is always in our midst; the transcendent always immanent, though our access to it may be blocked. Only the contemplative, capable of being surprised out of the complacency of ordinary seeing, appreciates the splendor of the simple and the hallowing of the everyday. Remaining in all its peculiarity and concreteness, this oak, dragonfly, molecule, or coyote—this student—reveals itself as redolent of Being. Every poet knows this, and every lover.

The unity and fluidity of the stages can be expressed as a holistic unity in the learner. It may be that we really have several "learners" in ourselves: we have our senses, which take in sense knowledge from the external world all the time; our minds, which reflect and process it; our hearts, which feel and value, appreciate or reject; and our deepest inner core, which some call the "soul," that which may be in tune with a finer, simpler, and greater reality than we meet in everyday consciousness. *Lectio divina's* contemplative learning challenges us to become sincere and integrated—one, not divided—with heart, hands, and head acting together, not duplicitous or hypocritical. This sincerity is simplicity: the contemplative's mind, like the child's, has room for wonder and for joy. She has become the child again, on the other side of the questioning, doubting, and debating that divide us from each other and ourselves. Contemplatives are inexorably happy people. They are the people for whom finding a four-leaf clover, a molecular reaction, a weaving of fine texture and delicate colors, or a single line of an exquisite poem literally makes their day. We don't see many of them in our schools and colleges.

Contemplation in Teaching: Transformation

Contemplation in all the stages of *lectio divina* transforms the reasoning and doubts of the reflective stage into hope and the desire that is the starting point of prayer into *love*. In place of the desire which seeks to master and to have the object, even in prayer, there is love and willingness. As Thomas Aquinas puts it, only love *transforms us* into the things that are in the mind, that desire has moved us toward.[3] The intellect has a drive to supersede itself, to go beyond seeing to union. But, since grace builds on nature, both the mind *and* its desire are necessary for this love to take root.

Contemplative Teaching and Transcendence

When we speak of transformation in teaching, we are opening a door to the transcendent. The notion of "transformation" is actually a religious one, for if we wanted to speak in more secular terms, we might call it developmental learning.[4] Transformation has little to do with the development that proceeds in a linear modality so that the student's "progress" can be charted. With transformation, these Enlightenment ideas fall to the ground, where the "seed grows, we know not how" (Mark 4:27). We can measure the distance we have come from ordinary teaching and learning by considering that instead of putting objects (or our students) off with a series of mental constructs in an effort to be "objective," or swallowing them up into our own subjectivity, we become what we love. Actually, the love we have opened ourselves to in making our teaching and learning contemplative also makes it transformative, for love is the most transforming power there is. A "we" emerges to replace the "they" of our students and the "I" of our ego.

Mystics have loved the imagery of fire for the final stage of transformation into the Beloved. In his *Living Flame of*

Love, John of the Cross's metaphor of a log enkindled until it becomes one living flame with the fire expresses the unifying power of transformation. In the spiritual alchemy of the log's burning, it becomes not only consumed but iridescent, itself emitting flames of acts of love, and of course this is a metaphor for the transformed soul: "All its acts are Divine, since it is impelled and moved to them by God."[5] Teresa of Avila in her *Interior Castle* also speaks of a heat being emitted from the fire of love and transmitted to others. Contemplation throughout the history of spirituality has involved a seeing that leads to communion with what is seen. In the Christian context, this *union* of two was not a monistic unity that effaced the otherness of the other, but a *unity in duality.* Contemplation of the world's variety, in scientific investigation or poetic musing, lets the other be other, without merging all in a mystical monism. In contemplating the world, sunflowers, goldfinches, chipmunks, and molasses remain. So, when we come to the "end" of the process, we are really at the beginning, that original unity that grounds us all.

The union achieved in contemplation respects but transcends the particularity and even the strangeness of the other. Contemplation is the middle way between atomism and narcissistic individualism on the one hand, and monistic blurring of the distinctive particularities of the world on the other hand. The stranger we welcome with our hospitality does not have to be assimilated to us, or rejected. Love keeps driving out fear. The receptivity we extend to the other is, in the vocabulary of the mystics, a *gelassenheit,* a letting-be or releasement of the other. Dualisms of self and world, which keep us separate, give way to the contemplative attitude of an interconnectedness, to love. Contemplation is the ideal way of relating in a pluralistic world. These are lofty statements, perhaps too lofty for the nitty-gritty grind of the classroom. What this means in our classrooms is the space to enjoy the pluralism of perspectives our students bring. Just when we give up on the need to convert them, they become converted—transformed—in their own way and time. Right there in that space and time, transformation happens.

Contemplative Teaching as Creativity

Like most moderns, we may see contemplation as the least practical and creative of the stages, so it helps to remember the origins of this term in the Western tradition. In Plato, Plotinus, and the later Christian writers, contemplation of the One, of God, was the most creative act of all, enabling the production of the World-Soul and all participant souls. These philosophers knew that gazing at the One empowered a person for the real work of creativity. The generativity or creativity of contemplation is one of its best-kept secrets. Contemplation shows us how to create from the most vital source of the universe, the Creative Spirit. To tap into this creative source is to initiate transformation that is in effect a re-creation of our selves and an emergence of our souls. Paradoxically, in using the Chinese philosopher Chuang Tzu's famous story of "The Woodcarver" as a symbol of the active life, Parker Palmer describes the process by which the woodcarver found the freedom to create a beautiful bell-stand as "a process of contemplation by which we penetrate the illusion of enslavement and claim our own inner liberty."[6] Today, finding and living from the place of soul gives us the passion to move into the world and to coax other souls out of hiding.

From "No" to "Yes"

Like all spiritual practice, contemplative teaching involves not-doing. To be contemplative in our teaching, we may need to say "no" to the many demands that only drain away our vitality. Contemplative teaching is the effortless seventh day, the Sabbath of the Spirit, the point where work becomes play. But we have to work very hard to get there! What is left out is *useless* activity, busyness for busyness' sake. David Whyte's *The Heart Aroused* tells the story of a group of Medical Missionary Sisters on a weekend retreat after years of exhausting work in the medical missions of Peru, Indonesia, India, and elsewhere.[7] Nearly all of these sisters had had no contemplative Sabbath for years to balance their totally depleting work. Only one, who had been a Poor Clare, a member of a strictly enclosed contemplative order, had learned how to say "no" as a path to soul. Her years of silent, prayerful life in the cloister had been a "no" to the claims of the world. Her series of "no's" actually constituted a dismantling of the false self.

Similarly, Martha is completed by Mary who just sat at Jesus' feet and listened (Luke 10:39–40), just as Mary gives Martha new life and energy for the work she must undertake. In Eckhart's version of this story, Mary turns back into Martha, "the virgin becomes a wife" and fruitful. "Out of those years of saying *no* blossomed a magnificent *yes*; magnificent because she would be nourishing much more than the physical health of those she would care for—a *yes* that could be followed fully because...every part of her would be uttering it. *Yes!*"[8] We teachers too can learn to say "no" to internal voices echoing the workaholism of our professions so that a more profound "yes" will appear.

At a point in my own professional teaching life, when I had split myself into two, doubling the number of committee meetings because of belonging to two (warring) departments, I resigned, and thereby said a huge "no." As each door closed with a thunderous thud, only a frightening vacuum seemed at first to be left. Yet, new doorways, opening onto more possibilities, began opening. Now I continue to struggle with teaching, but notice that it comes from a place not so much of duty as of hidden joy. Many "no's" over the years have been enfolded into this "yes." My definition of a good teacher—someone who agonizes over "bad days"—hasn't changed. But I have found with teaching, as Nietzsche said, that "joy is deeper yet than agony."

Transformed Teaching

All teachers implicitly feel that transformation is the goal of great teaching practice. Yet many feel that it is slipping away from us as an attainable or even a desirable goal; that we must reluctantly settle for the objective of getting students prepared for the battery (isn't this a term of assault?) of tests now being imposed on them and on us. Surely, if we teach contemplatively insofar as we get students to attend, to reflect, and to become receptive to others, we are doing exceedingly well. We are already part of the counterculture. Yet, teaching can be more than this. We can aim higher. The late English novelist and philosopher Iris Murdoch, realizing the need for a curriculum attentive to the inner life of students, pointed to the necessity of a meditative curriculum: "The damage done to inner life, to aloneness and quietness, through the imposition of banal or pornographic or violent images by television, is a considerable wound. Teach meditation in schools."[9] If she could say this in the first half of the twentieth century, how much more so today when far more banal, pornographic, and violent images flood our consciousness from myriad sources. This morning's *New York Times* carries the following comment in an editorial:

> There are many reasons that professors are uneasy talking of personal transformation, but a big one is the overall shift among universities to making the object of a liberal arts education not so much the development of the individual's inner life as it is the acquisition of skills.

> More and more we try to give our "customers" what they seem to want: marketable knowledge, powers that will hold them in good stead in the work force. Analytic powers are economically negotiable in ways that self-knowledge can't always be.[10]

This quotation is taken from an editorial titled "How Teachers Can Stop Cheating," with the double entendre that we teachers cheat our students as much as they turn to cheating when the inner life is neglected. When I see the response of my students to meditative time and to open dialogue, I wonder if they want only "marketable knowledge," if their higher self wants to be just a "customer."

Transformation cannot be controlled or verified; it does not show up on tests. To adopt a metaphor from the realm of "chaos theory," the "strange attractor" leading us into transformation through the chaos of conflict and disconfirmations does not have a lesson plan. In another powerful metaphor, transformation is birthing. When we talk about birthing, and the Western tradition of contemplation did this often in images such as Eckhart's "the birth of the Son in the soul," we are talking about transformation. Guigo the Carthusian also recognized that birthing is what we are about here: "But understanding will never cease *bringing this word [the son] to birth*, until faith is wholly transformed into the *sight* of God"[11] (italics added).

Transformative *teaching*, then, is midwifery, reaching into the soul of students to catch the bloody mess that is a new life. What the midwife, the spiritual director, and even the teacher can do is invite and encourage birth.[12] They cannot force it. There will still be unbirthed selves, as there are unlived lives. The midwife establishes a relationship of trust in which anything can be brought up, and no question is out of the question. The midwife has to know when it is appropriate simply to be with the birthgiver in pain and when to remind her that she has the power to help herself. As a new grandmother, I watched as a midwife skillfully delivered my grandsons, and I especially observed my daughter's trust and cooperation with her in the process of giving birth. Both mother and midwife were needed if birthing was to happen. This experience differed greatly from the birth of my own daughter, where the doctor did nearly all the work of delivery with a forceps (like standardized achievement tests!). To push the analogy just a bit further, the work of the midwife is not the doctor's forceps yanking the new life out of the womb, but patient, skillful tendering of this emerging life. Not interference, but *influence,* a natural overflow from the very being of the teacher-midwife herself, is the transformative force in teaching. I believe this influence is best described as *love,* not the sentimental kind that easily wears off, but the ontological kind that is simply there as a fundamental connection. The midwife "has time," unlike the overworked physician, and she can wait. As midwife-teachers, our primary ethic is an "ethic of presence."

When transformation is allowed to occur in our students—even if it seems outwardly only the birth of a paper or project—we teachers become midwives who wait in uncertainty, offer a patient, encouraging presence, coach the intense work of labor, and rejoice with them over the new life. Yet, we cannot do this work for students, just as we cannot "learn them"; we can only teach them, or really get out of the way and allow learning to go on, letting growth happen in the darkness of a rich soil, a dark but fertile inner life. But we are the ones who compost it!

There is death involved in transformation as well as new life. We can remember what Gregory says about Benedict's first students: that they "found it hard to let go of what they had thought about with their old minds in order to ponder new things."[13] Only at this point of transformation can the unquestioned assumptions and ideological fixations of our students (Benedict's "delusions of the devil") be abandoned. Only at this point can hardened hearts be softened, and even created anew, as in Ezekiel's "A new heart I will give you, and a new spirit I will put within you; and I will remove from your body the heart of stone and give you a heart of flesh" (Ezek 36:26). New hearts and new spirits. Ezekiel's metaphor is as radical as dying and rebirthing a self.

Transformation and Formation in Students

Transformation in our students, like the mystery of inner growth in stillness and darkness, is God's work. The seed grows, we know not how (Mark 4:27). Unless we operate with some sort of time-lapse camera in our heads, we may never see the transformation taking place in our students. When I sometimes hear from students about what they learned from a particular course, or how it turned them in a new direction, I am always amazed at how much more has happened than I or they were able to observe at the time. In 1967, just after the Second Vatican Council, Rosemary Haughton, an English housewife, wrote a prescient book foreseeing that the Catholic Church hung between the polarities of its business-as-usual *formation* process of educating people into doctrines and formulas (Baltimore Catechism style, I would surmise), and real *transformation* of the community of faith into discipleship. Rosemary Haughton's distinction between formation and transformation enables us to appreciate the radicality of transformation. Transformation, unlike formation, "is in the *in between;* it is unrelated, unstructured, eternal, self-sufficient, having no hierarchies, no morality, no past, no future, and no possibility of control." While *formation* is necessary to acculturate and socialize young people into the church, *transformation* "is total personal revolution," involving the "dissolution" of ordinary thinking and values, in effect the death of the person, and "birth of the whole human being."[14] Paradoxically, transformation happens only when formation *breaks down.*

Even if we are not in the business of religious transformation, we teachers need to ask whether our goal is merely to "form" students or to transform them, and be transformed ourselves. We need to ask whether we merely want students *conforming* to preexisting standards of thinking and behavior, or whether we are actually up for this more daunting process of transformation, or will at least not stand in its way. We need to confront our own fear of transformation in ourselves and in our students.

Transformation can be a lonely decision, one that at first separates a person from the supporting communal structures, not unlike the process of separation–initiation–reintegration required for a rite of passage from one state to another in ritual. Persons separate out from the community and from their accustomed roles (daughter, son, child, layperson), undergo the ritual initiation and teaching, and are reintegrated into the community with new identities (wife, husband, adult, prophet), often with new names. The emancipation afforded the person who undergoes transformation for the sake of the community lifts up the whole community, as in a shamanic or prophetic initiation. The prophetic call is a call to get beyond the idolatry of the status quo, a call to transformation. Ultimately, the prophetic voice, including the teacher who is willing to step out from the pack, can contribute to conditions for forming a more vital community–be it the class, the movement of teachers in a school seeking more authentic practice, or even wider "communities of congruence" (to use Parker Palmer's term) of those willing to transform education from within. Looking back to the civil rights movement, to Gandhi's armies of souls willing to suffer repeated beatings, to innovative teachers inspiring those who inspire others in turn, we can remind ourselves that transformed communities do and can exist, and that they begin with these prophets. In the last part of this chapter, we will look at some prophets of transformed communities.

When we allow for transformation, what gets transformed first in contemplative teaching is the classroom space—from a place where competition and fear, upstaging, and clever undercutting are the norm—to a place of genuine search and risk. It is a space where we—all of us, teachers and students—feel safe enough to be vulnerable. Such a space, though bounded, is open to the transcendent. To put it in theological terms, it is hospitable to the Holy Spirit. Like those waiting for the return of Elijah, we need to learn to "set a place" in our classrooms for the Holy Spirit's fire and energy of transformation. But like Elijah, we may need to learn that the Spirit's power is not always found in pyrotechnics; a great deal of contemplative teaching is about listening for the "still, small voices," voices of the Spirit that have not yet come to articulation in our students or in ourselves. This may especially be true in schools where students come from a home culture that silences their voices.

Transformation and Action in Schools

The call of transformation, whether to individuals or transformed communities, is a call to move us out into the world, to "walk the paths of peace and justice" (Prov 8:20). This is the call that our students need to hear, but only in concert with the other calls to reading, reflection, and receiving. I have said that contemplation is eminently practical, so I would like here to put contemplative teaching into practical terms.

Practically, this has meant for me "teaching around the circle."[15] I try to incorporate in my religious studies courses a learning cycle of *attention* as *concrete experiences* (CE), always readily available in the concrete forms and embodiments that religious experiences tend to take, but also in texts that ground us in the deeper meaning of our work; *reflection* as *reflective observations* (RO) that involve writing, dialogue, discussion, and silence in and out of the classroom on the meaning of the religious forms encountered, bringing about a contemplative focus to break the habit of multitasking; and *receptivity* as both *abstract conceptualization* (AC), appropriating for oneself in a Kierkegaardian way (that "truth is subjectivity") the theoretical and conceptual frameworks found in theology and philosophy and as heart connection through *active experimentation* (AE), where live encounter with others' religious values and symbols enables a deeper move into appropriation and connection and a potential *transformation.* As David Kolb, the creator of the learning styles inventory, puts it:

> [Students] must be able to involve themselves fully, openly, and without bias in new experiences (CE); they must be able to observe and reflect on these experiences from many perspectives (RO); they must be able to create concepts that integrate their observations into logically sound theories (AC); and they must be able to use these theories to make decisions and solve problems (AE)."[16]

Let me offer a couple of examples of this fourfold teaching approach. In my teaching of world religions, for example, I begin with *concrete experiences* that introduce students to the variety of stories, symbols, and practices abundantly evident in religions of Hinduism, Buddhism, or Islam. I use the notion of "practices" as a way into the concrete and material aspect of religion.[17] I make use of technological tools such as computer conversations and Web-links to enhance both the experiential and the reflective aspects of the religions. This Web-based methodology has tremendous potential to involve and excite more students where class size is greater than would be optimal. Through this methodology, we become a hermeneutic community, that is, a community of interpretation of symbols. We move toward *abstract conceptualization,* discovering a common vocabulary and constructing tentative conceptual frameworks to provide clarity for the abundant data we have been absorbing. Through these methods, theoretical concepts are not so much imposed as discovered. But especially in this point of the circle, we ask not only *what* a religious phenomenon is, but *how* is it true for me, *how* can I open my heart to it? The syllabus I designed for courses in world religions expresses the expectation that the student will take on the "challenge of confrontation with the *otherness* of Hinduism, Buddhism, Taoism, and Confucianism" and the familiarity of their "home-grown" religions in their many forms from ancient times to the present. I emphasize that the course involves an encounter requiring openness, intuition, and sympathy, one that allows the student to "pass over" to another religion's worldview and symbolism and to position themselves critically with regard to more familiar forms. This process of passing over is completed when the student is able to return to his or her own religion (substitute here literary tradition, historical time, or human experience if the course is biology) with greater understanding and appreciation. Finally, our goal is to engage in *active experimentation* with the religions themselves, at times involving field trips to mosques, synagogues, and Buddhist temples, participation in some form of service or ministry, or even a short monastic retreat.

Great "Transformers" and Students

Recently, I offered a course under the rubric "Great Humans in their Cultural Context," subtitled "100 Years of the Nobel Peace Prize." Here I attempted consciously or unconsciously to "teach around the circle" as my pedagogical approach. Our concrete experiences (and attention) began through the biographies and historical-cultural contexts of the Nobel laureates, enhanced by class presentations and role-playing by students. For many the encounter with Gandhi was new and compelling, overcoming the prejudice that peacemaking and nonviolence are impossible ideals. We looked long and hard at the nature of nonviolence (reflection) as we found it expressed in the lives and thought of the great peacemakers Gandhi and Martin Luther King, Jr. Through our computer conversations, class discussions, and presentations, we engaged in ongoing reflective observations that deepened our understanding of the significance of these figures. At the same time, we were beginning to ask the larger philosophical questions: Why is there war? Can there be a just war? What are the things that make for peace? Throughout the course, I raised questions of the origins and motivations for war. We looked closely at the tradition of just war, examining its principles of *jus ad bellum*, the conditions that must be met to wage war, as well as *jus in bello*, proportionality in the use of force, and prevention of civilian casualties.[18] Conceptually, peace and the positive concept of peace always seemed to be eluding our grasp. We came to the realization that concepts were not enough, but that only authentic encounters (receptivity) where people sit down together had the potential to overcome centuries of misunderstanding and hatred. We learned that peacemaking cannot be sketched out in abstract ideological schemes such as "road maps," but must be done through human beings in real face-to-face engagements. As mentioned previously, Kolb's stage of abstract conceptualization breaks down here, where the heart needs to open for real receptivity. These engagements with peacemakers often become "disorienting dilemmas" with "disconfirming others" that have transformative potential. Opportunities for active experimentation (AE), making our own decisions for action (transformation), became numerous in this atmosphere of build-up to the war in Iraq in 2002 when this course was offered.

The classroom itself was transformed and became permeable, as events found their way into the reflections of our students. Some of us began to flow out into marches and protests at what we perceived to be an unjust and unnecessary war. Our pedagogy was transformed: we drew images of nonviolence, strategized in small groups how to respond to hypothetical bullies, and role-played various Nobel Peace Prize laureates in dialogue with each other. On the day when Jimmy Carter was awarded the Nobel Peace Prize for 2002, our class had "ears to hear," especially to hear resonances of this award with those others we had studied.

In all these transformations, Gandhi was our guide, our prophetic voice. His own intellectual conversion took place in London in his reading of both the New Testament and the *Bhagavad Gita*. But his true moral transformation came with a jolt—a "disorienting dilemma"—when he was thrown off the train in South Africa.[19] For Gandhi, the stage of active experimentation meant "experiments with Truth," as he called his autobiography. He said it simply: "there are not many fundamental truths, but there is only one fundamental truth which is Truth itself, otherwise known as Nonviolence. Finite human being shall never know in its fullness Truth and love which is in itself infinite. But we do know enough for our guidance."[20] Gandhi's guidance by Truth became instructive to us. His dedication to nonviolence as a principle and his unstinting practice of it (his *satyagraha,* or "soul-force") over the rest of his life continued to inspire our students throughout the course.

We were witnesses to yet another transformation in this course, that of Martin Luther King, Jr. On his pilgrimage to nonviolence, King, like most of the students in the class, admitted that "like most people, [he] had heard of Gandhi, but had never studied him seriously." The Hindu became the critical teacher for King. Until he read Gandhi, he, like many Christians, had felt that the ethics of Jesus were applicable only in an individual context. Just when King had begun to despair of the power of love to solve social problems, Gandhi helped him overcome his skepticism. In King's words:

> Gandhi was probably the first person in history to lift the love ethic of Jesus above mere interaction between individuals to a powerful and effective social force on a large scale. Love, for Gandhi, was a potent instrument for social and collective transformation. It was in this Gandhian emphasis on love and nonviolence that I discovered the method for social reform that I had been seeking for so many months.[21]

Surprisingly, one of the great teachers in this course was failure! It taught us in the peace movement—those millions of people who got out in the streets in 2003 to protest the impending war on Iraq and did not succeed in stopping it—that the goal of the great peacemakers was not success but faithfulness. All the great peacemakers knew this, as they grabbed hold of truth and justice, not of the success their efforts might bring. They put themselves in relationship to holy power, *satya-graha,* the power or force of Truth, not expecting to use it but to be used by it. They knew the paradox that their very vulnerability and weakness opened them to sacred power making them a "channel for another kind of force"[22] than physical force. They knew also that nonviolence is another name for sacred power. Their contemplative life made them creative and powerful in the world.

This course was a kind of paradigm for me in learning to let go of ends, even the noble ends of transformation of students into peacemakers. Not everyone signed on to a program of nonviolence; not everyone was ready for this particular transformation. A few were. Let me share a couple of student reflections on the class:

> I came into this class in August with absolutely no idea that it was about the Nobel Peace Prize...when I saw the title, "Great Humans in their Cultural Context," I started thinking of Augustus Caesar and Joan of Arc. More far off, I could not be....This class has helped me further open my eyes to the idea that violence does not solve problems, and that peaceful resistance is a sign of intelligence and wisdom, not weakness.

One student even commented that his concrete experience of the subject matter had inspired him to follow in the footsteps of these leaders. He went on to say that before he took the class, the ideas of peace and nonviolence were mere words to him. "I understood a very general meaning and knew very little about the pioneers of such ideals," he said. Then understanding of the importance and reality of nonviolence followed (the second stage of *reflection*). By the end of the course, he had moved beyond understanding to a deep *receptivity* (the third stage) to these ideas and leaders. But he went even further to outline a plan for putting peace into action:

> It can start with people in this class reaching out to their friends and teaching them what they have learned. It can start by those of us in this class living a lifestyle conducive to promoting the ideals and notions of peace. It can start in the way we interact with our family and friends, then expand into our communities, and then reach the nation as a whole, and then hopefully spread across the world.

It is not inconsequential that this student began speaking of reaching out. The process of transformation changes not only the person, but the person's relationship to the world.

I realize that not everyone can be so fortunate as to teach a class where "great transformers" and noble and great ideas can actually translate into action. But with renewed interest in service-learning, term abroad programs, and internships, and even with the Internet, the classroom's boundaries are opening up to the world in some new and exciting ways. Like the monastery, its walls are permeable. When a panel of students was asked about their most life-altering experiences, nearly all of them pointed *outside* the classroom to mentoring, outward-bound, and volunteer activities—"extra-curricular" programs as they are often called. While more of these life-changing experiences can be given to students at all levels, the real question is whether they can also happen in the classroom. The challenge for us as teachers is to bring what is "extra" *inside,* to make the world concrete and accessible and therefore understandable to our students. We could say, paraphrasing Nicholas of Cusa (quoting other medieval writers), "the center is everywhere, the circumference is nowhere," and that " the classroom is everywhere, its circumference nowhere." The circle of *lectio divina,* when it becomes transformative, is one without circumference.

Epilogue: Transformation and Benedict's Conversatio Morum

"These, then, are the tools of the spiritual craft," Benedict states in the fourth chapter of his *Rule*.[1] As this book has been implicitly suggesting, we teachers too need to be converted, to undergo what Benedict called a *conversatio morum* or "conversion of manners," especially our manner of professionalism, so that we *see* our students as they are. Joan Chittister's words on the Benedictine spirituality of conversion are especially relevant to teachers: "What needs to be changed in us? Anything that makes us the sole center of ourselves. Anything that deludes us into thinking that we are not simply a work in progress, all of whose degrees, status, achievements, and power are no substitute for the wisdom that a world full of God everywhere, in everyone, has to teach us."[2] Let's face it: being a student, apprenticing yourself to another's wisdom and teachings, is making yourself vulnerable, even "woundable." If our students do that for us, we can reciprocate with our own vulnerability. Conversion means essentially growth in love. By some mysterious alchemy, the love of God in us as teachers, when it takes the form of love of our subjects, love of our students, and love of the very process of knowing and unknowing in which we are engaged, transforms *us* as teachers. God is our midwife too.

For me personally, the teaching of the course on the Nobel Peace Prize and the events surrounding it gave me an opening for transformation. I taught this course not so much from a knowledge base in the history of peacemaking, but from an ache that had been growing in me since the beginning of bombing in Afghanistan. I saw myself changing from a neutral observer of social and political events to an advocate for nonviolence. By the end of the course I had learned from my students that we must be *educated* to peace, to know what it is, to value it, and to embrace it. The course came to occupy the liminal space between learning and living, as I took to the streets for the Washington march and for local candlelight vigils and rallies. Yet, I was hardly prepared for the power of this kind of course to attack vestiges of cynicism in myself and some of the students. I was hardly prepared for hope! A broken link, between contemplation and action, study and application, was restored. My own evolution and transforming remains ongoing, and has taken ever new forms, making me more of an advocate for peace in my teaching.

As these examples imply, our own transformation gives us a vision of things we did not have before. Our transformed knowing is *vision,* a transcendent kind of knowing. The word *vision* implies an ability that is panoramic and far-ranging. We have vision from a mountaintop or down a long road opening out to the horizon. But an inner vision can see our path even when it winds in and out, up and down the valleys and hills, and even when the way darkens, because we don't really attain vision with our eyes but with our souls. Contemplation, simply put, is seeing in the dark, seeing with the light God shines into the dark of our destiny. St. John of the Cross, the sixteenth-century Spanish Carmelite mystic, taught that the dark night of the soul is actually the very light of God breaking into the situation. Although the "negative" experiences of impasse and darkness—of death to an old life and old habits of thinking—are central to contemplation, they are not the last word. "Impasse forces us to start all over again, driving us to contemplation....It forces the right side of the brain into gear, seeking intuitive, symbolic, unconventional answers, so that action can be renewed eventually with greater purpose."[3] In this statement we learn that contemplative beholding is not just seeing; its vision leads to becoming—to transformation. From a pedagogical perspective, the ethics of this insight involve the awareness that what we put in front of our students changes them.

How practical is contemplation in teaching, then, and what does contemplation have to do with teaching, as the question raised at the beginning of this book put it? Contemplation is the continuous lifelong practice of attention, reflection, receptivity, and vision toward what is really and uniquely there in our subject matters and in our students in all their opaqueness, complexity, uncertainty, and infinite variety. It is the practice of knowledge that transforms us through love and suffering and joy.

For a concluding view of teaching and contemplation, I believe we can look to Jesus and contemplate him in his role as a contemplative teacher. As teachers who want to be contemplatives, or as contemplatives who want to "share the fruits of contemplation" in teaching, Jesus is our teacher. That Jesus was a teacher is attested to in all the gospels, and indeed, *rabbi* is one of his most prominent titles. Jesus' parables are Zen *koans* of contemplative teaching. They say we must go through a darkness of intellectual understanding to get to the light of God's way of seeing things. The parables demand that people *see* a radically different reality, a reality turned upside down, where the lowly are lifted up and the poor blessed. They frustrate a merely conceptual grasp. In the hundredfold, the lost coin, the beneficent alien (Good Samaritan), they transcribe and evoke transformations.

If contemplation is awareness of the presence of God in all things, Jesus continually lived in that awareness and engaged others in and through it. Jesus invariably saw and attended to each person he encountered as an "image of God," reflections of God's immanent presence everywhere. In a typical encounter, when Jesus was asked by the rich young man what he must do to obtain eternal life, Jesus "looked on him and he loved him" (Mark 10:17–21), even when in other contexts he could be condemning of riches. Much of Mark's Gospel turns on the idea that some may "indeed look, but not perceive, and may indeed listen, but not understand"; and Jesus tells his disciples, "Pay attention to what you hear" (Mark 4:24). In his trial before the high priest and before Pilate, Jesus taught as much through silence as through his words. In John's Gospel, the most contemplative of all the gospels, Jesus teaches us to abide in him and in each other. That abiding and transforming love is the culmination of contemplation.

The contemplative way, the way of *lectio divina,* in teaching or any other ministry or relationship in crisis, is the way of attending-and-seeking in the darkness of the dark time, with faith that can barely be voiced because it sounds so absurd, with hope that a way through and beyond impasse will be found, and with whatever is left of love until that love is purified and emerges in new and integrated form. These are the "lessons" (literally "readings") of *lectio divina,* the faith of its attention to the world, the hope of its reflection on the world's mystery, and the transforming love that accompanies it all the way. They are the lessons and the play of contemplation, to be learned by both teachers and students, for all are learners when teaching is contemplative.

Notes

Introduction

1. Beginning with Parker Palmer's 1982 *To Know as We Are Known: Education as a Spiritual Journey* (San Francisco: Harper San Francisco, reprinted 1993), and more recently Mary Rose O'Reilley's *Radical Presence: Teaching as Contemplative Practice* (Portsmouth, NH: Boynton/Cook Publishers, 1998).

2. Parker Palmer, *The Courage to Teach: Exploring the Inner Landscape of a Teacher's Life* (San Francisco: Jossey-Bass Publishers, 1998).

3. See William T. Daly, "Teaching and Scholarship: Adapting American Higher Education," *The Journal of Higher Education* (Columbus, Jan. 1994); Paul C. Reinert, SJ, "The Catholic University's Recognition of Mystery," *America* (May 27, 1995), 25; Charles Glassick, "We Scholars: Changing the Culture of the University," Review of book by David Damrosch, *The Educational Record* (Winter 1996), 60; Peter Sacks, "No...Generation X is NOT OK," *The American Enterprise* (Jan/Feb 1998), 47; in William H. Willimon and Thomas H. Naylor, *The Abandoned Generation: Rethinking Higher Education* (New York: Wm. B. Eerdmans, 1995); Douglas, "Resolving the Crisis in Higher Education," *USA Today* (Jan. 1993), 83; Peter Brimelow, "Devalued Diplomas," *Forbes* (April 22, 1996), 156; Aaron W. Hughey, "Defining 'Quality' in Higher Education," *Louisville Courier-Journal* (Louisville, KY, Dec. 7, 1997), 04D.

4. Jürgen Habermas, *The Theory of Communicative Action: Reason and the Rationalization of Society*, Vol. 1, trans. Thomas McCarthy (Boston: Beacon Press, 1984).

5. Palmer, *To Know as We Are Known: Education as a Spiritual Journey*, 107.

6. We find the classic example of such thinking about education in Plato's *Meno*, where Socrates questions an uneducated slave boy so that the boy might discover that he already knows how to solve a problem in geometry.

7. Merton, "Learning to Live," in *Thomas Merton: Spiritual Master*, ed. with intro. by Lawrence S. Cunningham (New York/Mahwah, NJ: Paulist Press, 1992), 361.

8. From *Sermons on the Song of Songs,* quoted in Bernard, Abbot of Clairvaux, *The Steps of Humility,* trans. and with introduction by George Bosworth Burch (Notre Dame, IN: University of Notre Dame Press, 1963), 37.

9. See "Teaching and the Contemplative Life," in *Christian Spirituality Bulletin: Journal of the Society for the Study of Christian Spirituality*, Vol. 6, No. 2 (Fall 1998), 14–21 for the article from which this book developed.

10. Joan Chittister, *Illuminated Life: Monastic Wisdom for Seekers of Light* (Maryknoll, NY: Orbis Books, 2000), 76.

11. See Robert N. Sollod's article, "The Hollow Curriculum," in *The Chronicle of Higher Education* (March 18, 1992). Sollod's conclusion is a sad one: "[Students] learn either to suppress their spiritual life or to split their spiritual life apart from their formal education."

CHAPTER 1
Contemplation and Teaching

1. Saint John of the Cross, *Spiritual Canticle,* trans. E. Allison Peers (Garden City, NY: Image Books, 1961), 44.

2. Cf. Ephesians 1:18: "May he enlighten the eyes of your heart, so that you can see what hope his call holds for you, how rich is the glory of the heritage he offers among his holy people, and how extraordinarily great is the power that he has exercised for us believers."

Notes

3. For example, Daniel McGinn, "The Big Score," *Newsweek,* Vol. CXXXIV, No. 10 (September 6, 1999), 46–51.

4. See Mary Rose O'Reilley, *The Peaceable Classroom* (Portsmouth, NH: Boynton/Cook Publishers, 1993), chapter 5.

5. Thomas Merton, Asian Notes, Unpublished; quoted in John Miller, *The Contemplative Practitioner: Meditation in Education and the Professions* (Westport, CT: Bergin & Garvey, 1994), 114.

6. Columba Stewart, OSB, *Prayer and Community: The Benedictine Tradition* (Maryknoll, NY: Orbis Books, 1998), 22–23.

7. Ibid., 23–24.

8. This incident is described in St. Gregory's *Dialogues* (2.33) and discussed in *Prayer and Community,* 23.

9. Joan D. Chittister, OSB, *The Rule of Benedict: Insights for the Ages* (New York: Crossroad, 1998), 29.

10. *The Rule of Benedict,* "Prologue," 45.

11. *Prayer and Community,* 39.

12. From *The Notebooks of Malte Laurids Brigge,* trans. M. D. Herter Norton (201); quoted in Charles Cummings, OCSO, *Monastic Practices,* Cistercian Studies Series: No. 75 (Kalamazoo, MI Cistercian Publications, 1986), 9.

13. *Benedict's Dharma: Buddhists Reflect on the Rule of Saint Benedict,* ed. Patrick Henry (New York: Riverhead Books, 2001), 1.

14. "The Origin," Web site of the Grand Chartreuse, www.chartreux.org/eng/history1.htm.

15. See Samuel F. Weber, OSB, "Carthusian Spirituality," in *New Catholic Dictionary of Spirituality,* ed. Michael Downey (Collegeville, MN: The Liturgical Press, 1993), 125. You can still see these words, "God alone," on the gate of the Abbey of Gethsemane.

16. Statutes I.1, quoted in "The Origin," Web site of the Grand Chartreuse, www.chartreux.org/emg/history/.htm.

17. *Guigo II: Ladder of Monks and Twelve Meditations,* trans. with intro. by Edmund Colledge, OSA, and James Walsh, SJ (Kalamazoo, MI: Cistercian Pub., 1979), 3.

18. *Women and Teaching: Themes for a Spirituality of Pedagogy,* 1988 Madeleva Lecture in Spirituality (New York: Paulist Press, 1988), 14.

19. *Summa Theologiae,* II–III, Q. 188, Art. 6.

20. Ibid., II–II, Q. 180, Art. 7. This entire article is devoted to the question of whether there is delight in contemplation.

21. Ibid., II–II, Q. 180, Art. 4.

22. St. Teresa of Avila, *Interior Castle,* trans. E. Allison Peers (New York: Image Books, 1961), 81.

23. Sally Atkins, in *Expressive Arts Therapy: Creative Process in Art and Life* (Boone, NC: Parkway Publishers, Inc., 2003), 37.

24. Erich Auerbach's *Mimesis* (Princeton, NJ: Princeton University Press, 1953) makes this point brilliantly in chapter 2, "Fortunatus."

25. Parker Palmer speaks of the student writing an autobiography who asked if it was all right to use "I": *The Courage to Teach,* 18.

26. Thomas Merton, "Learning to Live," in *Thomas Merton: Spiritual Master,* 358.

27. Freire quotes Erich Fromm on the meaning of this term: "the necrophilous person loves all that does not grow, all that is mechanical....Memory, rather than experience; having, rather than being, is what counts" *Pedagogy of the Oppressed,* trans. Myra Bergman Ramos (New York: The Seabury Press, 1968), 64.

28. Margaret J. Wheatley, *Leadership and the New Science: Learning about Organization from an Orderly Universe* (San Francisco, CA: Berrett-Koehler, 1994).

29. Martin Buber, "Education," *Between Man and Man,* trans. Maurice Friedman (New York: Collier Books, 1955), 100.

30. Paulo Freire contrasts the banking method to "problem-posing education": "The teacher is no longer merely the-one-who-teaches, but one who is himself taught in dialogue with the students, who in turn while being taught also teach." *Pedagogy of the Oppressed,* 67.

31. From written personal questionnaires distributed by Connie Green, professor of Learning, Reading, and Exceptionalities, Appalachian State University, Boone, NC, November, 2001; used with permission.

32. See Sallie McFague's *Models of God: Theology for an Ecological, Nuclear Age* (Philadelphia: Fortress Press, 1987). See chapter 3 especially.

33. Impasse is actually another more contemporary name for the "dark night of the soul" as Constance FitzGerald, OCD, says in "Impasse and Dark Night" in *Living with Apocalypse* (New York: Harper & Row, 1984), 93–116; reprinted in *Women's Spirituality: Resources for Christian Development,* ed. Joann Wolski Conn (New York/Mahwah, NJ: Paulist Press, 1986), 287–311.

34. FitzGerald, "Impasse and Dark Night," 299.

35. William McNamara, *The Human Adventure* (Garden City, NJ: Doubleday, 1974); quoted in Robert J. Wicks, *Living Simply in an Anxious World* (Mahwah, NJ: Paulist Press, 1998), 82.

CHAPTER 2
Attention

1. This point is made eloquently by Ivan Illich's *In the Vineyard of the Text: A Commentary to Hugh's Didascalicon* (Chicago: University of Chicago Press, 1993). Hugh of St. Victor said this emphatically: "Unless God's wisdom is first known bodily you...cannot be enlightened for its spiritual contemplation. For this reason you must never look down upon the humility in which God's word reaches you. It is precisely this humility which will enlighten you." Quoted in Illich, 50.

2. *Ladder of Monks,* 83.

3. Ivan Illich, *Ivan Illich: In Conversation,* with David Cayley (Concord, Ontario: House of Anansi Press, 1992), 232. See *In the Vineyard of the Text.* Illich makes the simple observation that the parchment of twelfth-century books lit up the words and figures contained in them.

4. From Gerard Manley Hopkins' poem, "God's Grandeur," *The Poems of Gerard Manley Hopkins,* Fourth Edition, eds. W. H. Gardner and N. H. MacKenzie (Oxford: Oxford University Press, 1967), 66.

5. David Whyte, *The Heart Aroused: Poetry and the Preservation of the Soul in Corporate America* (New York: Doubleday, 1994), 23.

6. *Ladder of Monks,* 69.

7. Sharon Solloway, "Contemplative Practitioners: Presence, the Project of Thinking Gaze Differently," *Encounter*, Vol. 13, No. 3 (Autumn 2000), 30–42.

8. These experiments were conducted by John Miller, *The Contemplative Practitioner*, and further explored in Sharon Solloway, "Contemplative Practitioners."

9. Solloway says of mindfulness, "This transitional space-in-between is a pause, a momentary mixing with the chaos that exists before the naming, labeling, classifying aspects of language act to tame the world and make it known, and less threatening."

10. Thomas Merton, Asian Notes, Unpublished; quoted in John Miller, *The Contemplative Practitioner*, 114.

11. Miller, 11–13.

12. Ibid., 13.

13. Ibid., 16.

14. Ibid.

15. Solloway, 30–42.

16. Simone Weil, "Reflections on the Right Use of School Studies with a View to the Love of God," in *Waiting for God*, trans. Emma Craufurd (New York: Harper Colophon Books, 1951), 105–16.

17. All of these references can be found in Daphne Hampson, *After Christianity* (Valley Forge, PA: Trinity Press International, 1996), 260–62.

18. In her essay, "Reflections on the Right Use of School Studies with a View to the Love of God," Simone Weil finds the same thing: "If one says to one's pupils: 'Now you must pay attention,' one sees them contracting their brows, holding their breath, stiffening their muscles....The intelligence can only be led by desire. For there to be desire, there must be pleasure and joy in the work....The joy of learning is as indispensable in study as breathing in running. Where it is lacking, there are no real students, but only poor caricatures of apprentices who, at the end of their apprenticeship, will not even have a trade," 109–10.

19. Ibid., 112, 115.

20. "On 'God' and 'Good,'" in *The Sovereignty of Good* (New York: Schocken, 1971), 66; quoted in Donovan, 182.

21. "Reflections on the Right Use of School Studies," 114.

22. Emmanuel Levinas calls this an "ethics of allegiance to the other." See *Time and the Other,* trans. Richard A. Cohen (Pittsburgh, PA: Duquesne University Press, 1987), p. 8. Levinas states, "The 'relationship' from the ego to the other is thus asymmetrical....It is an awakening to the other person—the first arrival in his *proximity* as neighbor—irreducible to knowledge."

CHAPTER 3
Reflection

1. *Ladder of Monks,* 68 (see chap. 1, n. 17).
2. In a plenary address to the American Academy of Religion, November, 1998, Washington, D.C.
3. From Gregory the Great's *Gospel Homilies* (27;4; *Patrologia Latina* 76).
4. *Ladder of Monks,* 69.
5. Ibid., 80.
6. Ibid., 83.
7. Ibid., 71.
8. Laurence Freeman, OSB, "Meditation," in *The New Dictionary of Catholic Spirituality,* 649.
9. Michael Casey, OCSO, *Towards God: The Western Tradition of Contemplation* (Melbourne, Australia: Collins Dove, 1991), 74.
10. His translation of Rom. 1:21; *Ladder,* 72.
11. Antonio Damasio, "In the beginning was...Emotion," from *Looking for Spinoza: Joy, Sorrow, and the Feeling Brain,* in *Science and Spirit* (July–August 2003), 38–42.
12. Solloway remarks in her essay, "The capacity to think differently, to envision the unthinkable, is surrendered in exchange for experiencing the sign within the discipline of social conditioning or personal history. The opportunity to imagine something beyond the socially given slips away."
13. *Ladder of Monks,* 80.
14. William Shannon, "Contemplation," in the *New Dictionary of Catholic Spirituality,* 209.

15. Shirley Showalter and Jane Tompkins convened this session. Its subtitle was "A Collaborative Approach to Contemplative Teaching." July 25–28, 1996.

16. In Linda Lumsden, "Motivating Today's Students: The Same Old Stuff Just Doesn't Work," at http://eric.uoregon.edu/publications/text/portraits1.2.html.

17. Rosemary Haughton, *The Transformation of Man* [sic] (Springfield, IL: Templegate Pub., 1980), 176.

18. St. Teresa of Avila, *The Interior Castle,* trans. Kieran Kavanaugh, OCD, and Otilio Rodriguez, OCD, (New York/Mahwah, NJ: Paulist Press, 1979), 74.

19. *Ladder of Monks,* 71. Etty Hillesum describes her relationship with God using the image of a well: "There is a really deep well inside me. And in it dwells God. Sometimes I am there too. But more often stones and grit block the well, and God is buried beneath. Then He must be dug out again." *An Interrupted Life* (New York: Henry Holt and Co., 1996), 44.

20. Albert Einstein, "A Mathematician's Mind," in *Ideas and Opinions,* trans. Sonja Bargmann (New York: Bonanza Books, 1954), 25–26.

21. I am grateful to my husband and to the members of the American Association of Scientists for these examples of intuition in science.

22. Susanna Gal, associate professor of Biological Sciences, SUNY-Binghamton, NY; personal communication.

23. Meister Eckhart, "Sermon 52: Beati pauperes spiritu" in *Meister Eckhart: The Essential Sermons, Commentaries, Treatises, and Defense,* trans. and intro. by Edmund Colledge, O.S.A. and Bernard McGinn (New York/Mahwah, NJ: Paulist Press, 1981), 200.

24. By Jonathan Bronner, "Response to War/Levertov," March 20, 2003, on Web-CT, http://cni3.appstate.edu:8900/SCRIPT/1398020041/scripts/serve_home.

25. See Maria Lichtmann, "Marguerite Porete's Mirror for Simple Souls: Inverted Reflection of Self, Society, and God," in *Studia Mystica,* Vol. XVI, No. 1 (1995): 4–29.

26. Sr. Ritamary Bradley, in an article on the concept of mirror in the Middle Ages, (*Speculum* 29, [1954]: 100–19), discusses

the mirror's "double function of showing the world what it is and what it should become."

27. Solloway, "Contemplative Practitioners."

28. From Ann Solberg, Berea College's "Communication Across the College" Web page, www.berea.edu/CAC/CAC5/RR98AS.HTML.

29. *Ladder of Monks,* 72.

30. Albert Einstein, "The World as I See It," in *Ideas and Opinions* (New York: Bonanza Books, 1954), 11.

31. Philip Hallie, *Lest Innocent Blood Be Shed: The Story of the Village of Le Chambon and How Goodness Happened There* (New York: HarperPerennial, 1994).

CHAPTER 4
Receptivity

1. *Ladder of Monks,* 73.

2. Palmer, *To Know as We Are Known,* 18.

3. Thomas Merton critiques this idea of prayer: "Prayer in the context of this inner awareness of God's direct presence becomes not so much a matter of cause and effect, as a celebration of love....Celebration and praise, loving attention to the presence of God, become more important than 'asking for' things and 'getting' things," in *Thomas Merton: Spiritual Master,* 373.

4. Palmer, *To Know as We Are Known,* 11.

5. From Latin *precare,* "to entreat or beg"; cf. Hebrew *pālal,* "to mediate or intercede" and *tsela,* "to bow or bend down," and Greek *proeuchomai,* "wish or vow toward."

6. C. S. Lewis, *Till We Have Faces* (Grand Rapids, MI: Eerdmans Publishing Co., 1960), 294.

7. *Ladder of Monks,* 72.

8. Ibid., 71–72.

9. Ibid., 124.

10. Ibid., 69.

11. Thomas Merton, *The Asian Journal of Thomas Merton* (New York: New Directions, 1975), 307.

12. Martin Buber, "Education," *Between Man and Man,* 91.

13. David Kolb, *Experiential Learning: Experience as the Source of Learning and Development* (Englewood Cliffs, NJ: Prentice-Hall, 1984).

14. Chittister, *Illuminated Life*, 129.

15. Chittister, *Rule of St. Benedict*, 142.

16. *The Poems of Gerard Manley Hopkins,* Fourth Edition, eds. W. H. Gardner and N. H. MacKenzie (Oxford: Oxford University Press, 1970), 53.

17. Henri Nouwen, *Reaching Out: The Three Movements of the Spiritual Life* (New York: Doubleday and Co., 1975), 61.

18. *The Rule of Benedict*, 141.

19. *The Rule of Benedict*, 90.

20. Jane Tompkins, "Pedagogy of the Distressed," *College English,* Vol. 52, No. 6 (Oct. 1990), 653–60.

21. Joan Chittister compares this Benedictine greeting to the Hindu greeting "Namaste," meaning, "I honor the place in you where the entire universe resides; I honor the place in you of love, of light, of truth, of peace. I honor the place within you where if you are in that place in you and I am in that place in me, there is only one of us." *Rule of Benedict*, 141.

22. Ibid., 129–130.

23. *Illuminated Life*, 127.

24. Robert Coles, *The Call of Stories* (New York: Houghton Mifflin Co., 1989), 129.

25. http://ublib.buffalo.edu/libraries/projects/cases/case.html. I am grateful to Susannah Gal, associate professor of Biological Sciences, SUNY-Binghamton, NY, for this comment and her referring me to the case study method in science.

26. This term is Jack Mezirow's in *Transformative Dimensions of Adult Learning* (New York: John Wiley & Sons, 1991), 169.

27. This phrase is Jonathan Z. Smith's.

28. See *Transformative Dimensions of Adult Learning,* 169.

29. Thomas Merton, *Gandhi on Non-Violence,* ed., and with introduction by Thomas Merton (New York: New Directions, 1964), 12.

30. Solloway speaks of "the miracle of voices speaking themselves in our gaze more closely as themselves—a radical form of

caring." The quotation is from D. Abram, *The Spell of the Sensuous* (New York: Vintage Books, 1996), 81.

31. Jacques Dupuis, SJ, *Toward a Christian Theology of Religious Pluralism* (Maryknoll, NY: Orbis, 1997), 382–83, says, "The encounter and exchange have value in themselves....While, to begin with, they presupposed openness to the other and to God, they also effect a deeper openness to God of each through the other....[The dialogue] tends to a more profound conversion of each to God."

32. Haughton, *The Transformation of Man*, 155, 244.

33. *The Rule of St. Benedict,* chaps. 53, 89.

34. Chapter 20, "Reverence in Prayer," in Joan D. Chittister, OSB, *The Rule of Benedict,* 90.

35. In Parker Palmer, *To Know As We Are Known,* 10.

36. *The Rule of Benedict,* chapter 53.

CHAPTER 5
Transformation and Action

1. *Ladder of Monks,* 79–80.

2. Michael Casey, *Sacred Reading: The Ancient Art of Lectio Divina* (Liguori, MO: 1996), 58.

3. "Exposition," *De Divinis Nominibus,* ii, lect. 4; in *Philosophical Texts,* Selected by Thomas Gilby (Durham, NC: The Labyrinth Press, 1982), 33.

4. As Rosemary Haughton sees it, whatever explicitly directs secular life toward transformation can be called "religious." Haughton, *The Transformation of Man,* 247.

5. St. John of the Cross, *Living Flame of Love,* trans. and ed. by E. Allison Peers (New York: Doubleday & Co., 1962), 155.

6. Parker Palmer, *The Active Life: Wisdom for Work, Creativity, and Caring* (San Francisco: HarperCollins, 1991), 60.

7. *The Heart Aroused: Poetry and the Preservation of the Soul in Corporate America* (New York: Doubleday, 1994), 139–43.

8. Ibid., 141.

9. From *Metaphysics as a Guide to Morals* (London: Chatto & Windus), 337; quoted in John Miller, *Education and the Soul,* 50.

10. Mark Edmundsen, "How Teachers Can Stop Cheating," *New York Times*, September 9, 2003. Edmundsen goes on to say that one reason so many essays are plagiarized today is their distance from the personal inner lives of students.

11. *Meditation* X, 121.

12. Margaret Guenther has written a beautiful book on spiritual direction called *Holy Listening* in which she describes the spiritual director as midwife to the soul: Margaret Guenther, *Holy Listening: The Art of Spiritual Direction* (Cambridge, MA: Cowley Publications, 1992). Much of what she says of the spiritual director can be said of the teacher, whom we have already compared to the "spiritual friend."

13. Ibid., 23–24.

14. Rosemary Haughton, *The Transformation of Man*. See especially chapter 8, "The Meaning of the Church," 242–80. Although the context in which she makes these remarks is faith development, they can apply just as much to the wider process of learning.

15. Based on the work of David Kolb, with the modifications cited earlier.

16. David Kolb, "Learning Styles and Disciplinary Differences," in Arthur W. Chickering and Associates, *The Modern American College* (San Francisco: Jossey-Bass, 1981), 236.

17. Using Robert Wuthnow's examination of the contemporary American landscape of spirituality, in *After Heaven: Spirituality in America Since the 1950s* (Berkeley: University of California Press, 1998).

18. See William V. O'Brien, "The Conduct of Just and Limited War," in *Approaches to Peace: A Reader in Peace Studies*, ed. David P. Barash (New York: Oxford University Press, 2000), 80–85.

19. See Louis Fischer, *Gandhi: His Life and Message for the World* (New York: New American Library, 1954), 22.

20. From http://www.mkgandhi.org/philosphy/index.htm.

21. Martin Luther King, Jr., "My Pilgrimage to Nonviolence," in *Peace Is the Way: Writings on Nonviolence from the Fellowship*

of Reconciliation, ed. Walter Wink (Maryknoll, New York: Orbis Books, 2002), 68.

22. The phrase is from A. J. Muste's "The Pacifist Way of Life," in *Peace Is the Way* 30–36.

Epilogue:
Transformation and Benedict's Conversatio Morum

1. *The Rule of Benedict: Insights for the Ages,* 56.
2. Chittister, *Illuminated Life,* 81–82.
3. Belden Lane; quoted in FitzGerald, OCD, "Impasse and Dark Night," 93–116.

For Further Reading

INTRODUCTION AND CHAPTER 1

Aelred of Rievaulx. *Spiritual Friendship,* trans. Mark F. Williams. Scranton, PA: University of Scranton Press, 1994.

Allen, George. *Rethinking College Education.* Lawrence, Kansas: University Press of Kansas, 1997.

Bass, Dorothy, ed. *Practicing Our Faith: A Way of Life for a Searching People.* San Francisco, CA: Jossey-Bass, 1997.

Brookfield, Stephen D. *Becoming a Critically Reflective Teacher.* San Francisco, CA: Jossey-Bass Publishers, 1995.

Buber, Martin. *Between Man and Man,* intro. by Maurice Friedman. New York: Collier Books, 1955.

Chittister, Joan, OSB. *Illuminated Life: Monastic Wisdom for Seekers of Light.* Maryknoll, NY: Orbis Books, 2000.

Coles, Robert. *The Call of Stories: Teaching and the Moral Imagination.* Boston: Houghton Mifflin Company, 1989.

Cummings, Charles, OCSO. *Monastic Practices.* Cistercian Studies Series No. 75. Kalamazoo, MI: Cistercian Publications, 1986.

Ellsberg, Robert. *All Saints: Daily Reflections on Saints, Prophets, and Witnesses for Our Time.* New York: Crossroad, 1997. On Aquinas.

FitzGerald, Constance, OCD. "Impasse and Dark Night," in *Living with Apocalypse.* New York: Harper & Row, 1984; reprinted in Joann Wolski Conn, ed. *Women's Spirituality: Resources for Christian Development.* New York/Mahwah, NJ: Paulist Press, 1986, 410–35.

Freire, Paulo. *Pedagogy of the Oppressed,* trans. Myra Bergman Ramos. New York: The Seabury Press, 1968.

Guigo II: Ladder of Monks and Twelve Meditations, trans. with introduction by Edmund Colledge, OSA, and James Walsh, SJ, editors. *Meister Eckhart.* Kalamazoo, MI: Cistercian Publications, 1979.

hooks, bell. *Teaching to Transgress: Education as the Practice of Freedom.* New York: Routledge, 1994.

Magid, Shaul. "Monastic Liberation as Counter-Cultural Critique in the Life and Thought of Thomas Merton." *Cross Currents* 49, No. 4 (Winter 1999–2000): 445–62.

McFague, Sallie. *Models of God: Theology for an Ecological, Nuclear Age.* Philadelphia, PA: Fortress Press, 1987.

Merton, Thomas. From *Conjectures of a Guilty Bystander,* in *Thomas Merton: Spiritual Master,* ed. with intro. by Lawrence S. Cunningham. New York/Mahwah, NJ: Paulist Press, 1992, 121–64.

———. "The Inner Experience," in *Thomas Merton: Spiritual Master,* ed. with intro. by Lawrence S. Cunningham. New York/Mahwah, NJ: Paulist Press, 1992, 294–356.

———. "Learning to Live," in *Thomas Merton: Spiritual Master,* ed. with intro. by Lawrence S. Cunningham. New York/Mahwah, NJ: Paulist Press, 1992, 357–67.

Miles, Margaret. *Practicing Christianity: Critical Perspectives for an Embodied Spirituality.* New York: Crossroad Publications, 1990.

———. *The Rule of Benedict: Insights for the Ages.* New York: Crossroad, 1998.

Miller, John. *The Contemplative Practitioner: Meditation in Education and the Professions.* Westport, CT: Bergin & Garvey, 1994.

O'Reilley, Mary Rose. *The Peaceable Classroom.* Portsmouth, NH: Boynton/Cook Publishers, 1993.

———. *Radical Presence: Teaching as Contemplative Practice.* Portsmouth, NH: Boynton/Cook Publications, 1998.

Palmer, Parker. *To Know as We Are Known: Education as a Spiritual Journey.* San Francisco: HarperSanFrancisco, 1982 and 1993.

———. *The Courage to Teach: Exploring the Inner Landscape of a Teacher's Life.* San Francisco: Jossey-Bass, 1998.

Pennington, M. Basil, OCSO. "Monasticism, Monastic Spirituality," in *New Dictionary of Catholic Spirituality*, ed. Michael Downey. Collegeville, MN: Liturgical Press, 1993.

Shannon, William. "Contemplation, Contemplative Prayer," in *New Dictionary of Catholic Spirituality*, ed. Michael Downey. Collegeville, MN: Liturgical Press, 1993.

Sollod, Robert N. "The Hollow Curriculum." *The Chronicle of Higher Education* (March 18, 1992).

Stewart, Columba, OSB. *Prayer and Community: The Benedictine Tradition*. Maryknoll, NY: Orbis Books, 1998.

St. Thomas Aquinas, *Summa Theologiae*, II–III, Q. 188, Art. 6. See http://www.newadvent.org/summa/3.htm.

Tompkins, Jane. *A Life in School: What the Teacher Learned*. Reading, MA: Addison-Wesley Publishing Co., 1996.

Weber, Samuel F., OSB. "Carthusian Spirituality," in *New Dictionary of Catholic Spirituality*, ed. Michael Downey. Collegeville, MN: Liturgical Press, 1993.

Web site of the Grand Chartreuse, http://www.chartreux.org/eng/history1.htm.

Wright, Wendy. "'A Wide and Fleshly Love': Images, Imagination, and the Study of Christian Spirituality." *Christian Spirituality Bulletin* 7, No. 1 (Spring 1999).

Wuthnow, Robert. *After Heaven: Spirituality in America Since the 1950s*. Berkeley, CA: University of California Press, 1998.

CHAPTER 2

Donovan, Josephine. *Feminist Theory: The Intellectual Traditions of American Feminism*. New York: Continuum, 1990.

Guigo II: Ladder of Monks and Twelve Meditations, trans. with introduction by Edmund Colledge, OSA, and James Walsh, SJ, eds. *Meister Eckhart*. Kalamazoo, MI: Cistercian Publications, 1979.

Harris, Maria. *Women and Teaching: Themes for a Spirituality of Pedagogy*, 1988 Madeleva Lecture in Spirituality. New York/Mahwah, NJ: Paulist Press, 1988.

Illich, Ivan. *In the Vineyard of the Text: A Commentary to Hugh's Didascalicon*. Chicago: University of Chicago Press, 1993.

Miller, John. *The Contemplative Practitioner: Meditation in Education and the Professions.* Westport, CT: Bergin and Garvey, 1994.

Murdoch, Iris. "On 'God' and 'Good,'" in *The Sovereignty of Good.* New York: Schocken, 1971.

St. Teresa of Avila, *Interior Castle,* trans. E. Allison Peers. New York: Image Books, 1961.

Underhill, Evelyn. *Mysticism.* New York: E. P. Dutton, 1961.

Weil, Simone. "Reflections on the Right Use of School Studies with a View to the Love of God," in *Waiting for God,* trans. Emma Craufurd. New York: Harper Colophon Books, 1951.

Wheatley, Margaret J. *Leadership and the New Science: Learning about Organization from an Orderly Universe.* San Francisco, CA: Berrett-Koehler, 1994.

Wuthnow, Robert. *After Heaven: Spirituality in America Since the 1950s.* Berkeley, CA: Univ. of California Press, 1998.

Whyte, David. *The Heart Aroused: Poetry and the Preservation of the Soul in Corporate America.* New York: Doubleday, 1994.

CHAPTER 3

Bouyer, Louis. *Introduction to Spirituality,* trans. Mary Perkins Ryan. Collegeville, MN: Liturgical Press, 1961.

Buber, Martin. "Education," in *Between Man and Man,* trans. Ronald Gregor Smith. Boston: Beacon Press, 1955.

Casey, Michael, OCSO. *Towards God: The Western Tradition of Contemplation.* Melbourne, Australia: Collins Dove, 1991.

Chittister, Joan, OSB. *Rule of St. Benedict: Insights for the Ages,* Chapter 53. New York: Crossroad, 1998.

Einstein, Albert. "The World as I See It," in *Ideas and Opinions,* trans. Sonja Bargmann. New York: Bonanza Books, 1954.

Freeman, Laurence, OSB. "Meditation," in *The New Dictionary of Catholic Spirituality,* ed. Michael Downey. Collegeville, MN: Liturgical Press, 1993.

Guigo II: Ladder of Monks and Twelve Meditations, trans. with introduction by Edmund Colledge, OSA, and James Walsh, SJ, eds. *Meister Eckhart.* Kalamazoo, MI: Cistercian Publications, 1979.

Illich, Ivan. *In the Vineyard of the Text: A Commentary to Hugh's Didascalicon.* Chicago: University of Chicago Press, 1993.

Kolb, David. *Experiential Learning: Experience as the Source of Learning and Development.* Englewood Cliffs, NJ: Prentice-Hall, 1984.

Leclercq, Jean, OSB. *The Love of Learning and the Desire for God: A Study of Monastic Culture,* trans. Catharine Misrahi. New York: Fordham University Press, 1961.

Levinas, Emmanuel. *Time and the Other,* trans. Richard A. Cohen. Pittsburgh, PA: Duquesne University Press, 1987.

Miller, John. *The Contemplative Practitioner: Meditation in Education and the Professions.* Westport, CT: Bergin & Garvey, 1994.

————. "Contemplative Practice in Higher Education: An Experiment in Teacher Development," in *Journal of Humanistic Psychology* 34, No. 4, (Fall 1994): 53–69.

Shannon, William. "Contemplation," in the *New Dictionary of Catholic Spirituality,* ed. Michael Downey. Collegeville, MN: Liturgical Press, 1993.

Solloway, Sharon. "Contemplative Practitioners: Presence, the Project of Thinking Gaze Differently." *Encounter* 13, No. 3 (Autumn 2000): 30–42.

CHAPTER 4

Buber, Martin. "Education," in *Between Man and Man,* trans. Ronald Gregor Smith. Boston: Beacon Press, 1955.

Casey, Michael. *Sacred Reading: The Ancient Art of Lectio Divina.* Liguori, MO: 1996.

Chittister, Joan D., OSB. Chapter 20, "Reverence in Prayer," in *The Rule of Benedict: Insights for the Ages.* New York: Crossroad, 1998.

————. *Illuminated Life: Monastic Wisdom for Seekers of Light.* Maryknoll, NY: Orbis Books, 2000.

Coles, Robert. *The Call of Stories: Teaching and the Moral Imagination.* Boston: Houghton Mifflin Company, 1989.

Csikszentmihaly, Mihaly. *The Psychology of Optimal Experience.* New York: Harper Collins, 1990.

For Further Reading

Dupuis, Jacques, SJ, *Toward a Christian Theology of Religious Pluralism*. Maryknoll, NY: Orbis, 1997.

Edmundsen, Mark. "How Teachers Can Stop Cheating." *New York Times* (September 9, 2003).

Guenther, Margaret. *Holy Listening: The Art of Spiritual Direction*. Cambridge, MA: Cowley Publications, 1992.

Guigo II: Ladder of Monks and Twelve Meditations, trans. with introduction by Edmund Colledge, OSA, and James Walsh, SJ, eds. *Meister Eckhart*. Kalamazoo, MI: Cistercian Publications, 1979.

Harris, Maria. *Teaching and Religious Imagination: An Essay in the Theology of Teaching*. San Francisco: HarperCollins, 1991.

Haughton, Rosemary. *The Transformation of Man* [sic]. Springfield, IL: Templegate Publishers, 1980.

Kolb, David. *Experiential Learning: Experience as the Source of Learning and Development*. Englewood Cliffs, NJ: Prentice-Hall, 1984.

Merton, Thomas. *Gandhi on Non-Violence,* ed. and with introduction by Thomas Merton. New York: New Directions, 1964.

―――. *The Asian Journal of Thomas Merton*. New York: New Directions, 1975.

Mezirow, Jack. *Transformative Dimensions of Adult Learning*. New York: John Wiley & Sons, 1991.

Nouwen, Henri. *Reaching Out: The Three Movements of the Spiritual Life*. New York: Doubleday and Co., 1975.

Palmer, Parker. *To Know as We Are Known: Education as a Spiritual Journey*. San Francisco: Harper San Francisco, 1982 and 1993.

―――. *The Active Life: Wisdom for Work, Creativity, and Caring*. San Francisco: HarperCollins, 1991.

Rose, Mike. *Lives on the Boundary*. New York: Penguin, 1990.

Solloway, Sharon. "Contemplative Practitioners: Presence, the Project of Thinking Gaze Differently." *Encounter* 13, No. 3 (Autumn 2000), 30–42.

St. Teresa of Avila, *The Interior Castle,* trans. Kieran Kavanaugh, OCD, and Otilio Rodriguez, OCD. New York/Mahwah, NJ: Paulist Press, 1979.

Tompkins, Jane. "Pedagogy of the Distressed." *College English* 52, No. 6 (Oct. 1990), 653–60.

Whyte, David. *The Heart Aroused: Poetry and the Preservation of the Soul in Corporate America.* New York: Doubleday, 1994.

CHAPTER 5

Barash, David P., ed. *Approaches to Peace: A Reader in Peace Studies.* New York: Oxford University Press, 2000.

Brancatelli, Robert. "Discipleship and the Logic of Transformative Catechesis," in *Spirit Church, and World. The Annual Publication of the College Theology Society,* Vol. 49. ed. Bradford Hinze. Maryknoll, NY: Orbis Books, 2003.

Buchmann, Margret. "The Careful Vision: How Practical Is Contemplation in Teaching?" Michigan State University: The National Center for Research on Teacher Education, March 1989, and at http://ncrtl.msu.edu./http/ipapers/html/pdf/ip891.pdf.

Casey, Michael. *Sacred Reading: The Ancient Art of Lectio Divina.* Liguori, MO: Liguori Press, 1996.

Chittister, Joan. *Wisdom Distilled from the Daily: Living the Rule of St. Benedict Today.* San Francisco, CA: HarperCollins, 1990.

Fischer, Louis. *Gandhi: His Life and Message for the World.* New York: New American Library, 1954.

Harris, Maria. *Teaching and Religious Imagination: An Essay in the Theology of Teaching.* San Francisco: HarperCollins, 1991.

King, Martin Luther, Jr. "My Pilgrimage to Nonviolence," in *Peace Is the Way: Writings on Nonviolence from the Fellowship of Reconciliation,* ed. Walter Wink. Maryknoll, NY: Orbis Books, 2002.

Kolb, David. "Learning Styles and Disciplinary Differences," in Chickering, Arthur W. and Associates, *The Modern American College.* San Francisco: Jossey-Bass, 1981.

Merton, Thomas. *The Asian Journal of Thomas Merton.* New York: New Directions, 1975.

Miller, John. *The Contemplative Practitioner.* San Francisco: Jossey-Bass, 1995.

For Further Reading

———. *Education and the Soul: Toward a Spiritual Curriculum.* With a Foreword by Thomas Moore. Albany, NY: State University of New York Press, 2000.

Palmer, Parker. "Divided No More: Teaching from a Heart of Hope," chapter 5, in *The Courage to Teach*. San Francisco, CA: Jossey-Bass Inc., 1998.

Schulz, Mona Lisa. *Awakening Intuition: Using Your Mind-Body Network for Insight and Healing.* New York: Three Rivers Press, 1998.

Soelle, Dorothy. *The Silent Cry: Mysticism and Resistance,* trans. Barbara and Martin Rumscheidt. Minneapolis: Fortress Press, 2001.

Wink, Walter, ed. *Peace Is the Way: Writings on Nonviolence from the Fellowship of Reconciliation.* Maryknoll, NY: Orbis Books, 2002.